Mode of Production

Historical Materialism Book Series

The Historical Materialism Book Series is a major publishing initiative of the radical left. The capitalist crisis of the twenty-first century has been met by a resurgence of interest in critical Marxist theory. At the same time, the publishing institutions committed to Marxism have contracted markedly since the high point of the 1970s. The Historical Materialism Book Series is dedicated to addressing this situation by making available important works of Marxist theory. The aim of the series is to publish important theoretical contributions as the basis for vigorous intellectual debate and exchange on the left.

The peer-reviewed series publishes original monographs, translated texts, and reprints of classics across the bounds of academic disciplinary agendas and across the divisions of the left. The series is particularly concerned to encourage the internationalization of Marxist debate and aims to translate significant studies from beyond the English-speaking world.

For a full list of titles in the Historical Materialism Book Series available in paperback from Haymarket Books, visit: www.haymarketbooks.org/series_collections/1-historical-materialism.

Mode of Production

The Final Horizon of Practice and Theory

Henry Heller
Peter Kulchyski

Haymarket Books
Chicago, IL

First published in 2025 by Brill Academic Publishers, The Netherlands

Published in paperback in 2026 by
Haymarket Books
P.O. Box 180165
Chicago, IL 60618
773-583-7884
www.haymarketbooks.org

ISBN: 979-8-88890-890-7

Distributed to the trade in the US through Consortium Book Sales and Distribution (www.cbsd.com) and internationally through Ingram Publisher Services International (www.ingramcontent.com).

This book was published with the generous support of Lannan Foundation, Wallace Action Fund, and the Marguerite Casey Foundation.

Art and design by David Mabb. Cover art is a development from *Construct 36, Morris, Willow Boughs / Rodchenko Fabric Design*. Pen and paint on wallpaper (2006).

Printed in the United States.

Library of Congress Cataloging-in-Publication data is available.

History is what hurts, it is what refuses desire and sets inexorable limits to individual as well as collective praxis, which its 'ruses' turn into grisly and ironic reversals of their overt intention. But this History can be apprehended only through its effects, and never directly as some reified force. This is indeed the ultimate sense in which History as ground and untranscendable horizon needs no particular theoretical justification: We may be sure that its alienating necessities will not forget us, however much we might prefer to ignore them.

FREDRIC JAMESON

Contents

Preface XI

Introduction 1

1 **Concerning a Concept** 9
- 1 An Ancient Trail through the Forest of Thought 10
- 2 Mode of Production in the History of Theory 14
- 3 Mode of Production in the Contemporary Theoretical Moment 23
- 4 Three Modes of Production: Prefatory Description 26
- 5 Final Thoughts for a First Chapter 30
- 6 Source Note 35

2 **Capitalism** 36
- 1 The Capitalist Relation 37
- 2 Origins and Primitive Accumulation 39
- 3 Value 40
- 4 The World Market 41
- 5 Uneven Development 42
- 6 Phases of Capitalism 42
- 7 Merchant Capitalism 43
- 8 State and Church 44
- 9 Gender 45
- 10 The Politics of Uneven Development 46
- 11 Colonialism 46
- 12 Resistance 48
- 13 Revolution 49
- 14 Industrial Revolution and Development of the Working Class 50
- 15 Free Labour 51
- 16 Monopoly Capitalism 53
- 17 Revolution in Russia 54
- 18 Actually Existing Socialism 55
- 19 Fascism and War 57
- 20 U.S. Hegemony and the Cold War 58
- 21 Neoliberalism 58
- 22 Source Note 61

3 **The Tributary Mode of Production and Capitalism** 62
1 The Tributary Mode and Capitalism 64
2 Neolithic Inheritances 65
3 Asiatic Mode of Production 67
4 The Other Transition 70
5 The Mediaeval Period 70
6 Late Mediaeval Crisis 71
7 Early Modern Feudalism 72
8 Slavery 73
9 The State and the Tributary Mode 76
10 The Tributary Mode: Critique 78
11 Source Note 80

4 **The Bush Mode of Production** 81
1 Introduction 81
2 The Civilised/Savage Dichotomy 82
3 Features of the Bush Mode of Production I: Egalitarianism 83
4 Features of the Bush Mode of Production II: Communism 86
5 Features of the Bush Mode of Production III: Nomadism 87
6 Features of the Bush Mode of Production IV: Affluence 88
7 Features of the Bush Mode of Production V: Expressive Culture and Spirituality 89
8 The Global History of the Bush Mode of Production 90
9 Bush History and Bush Culture: A Few Comments 93
9.1 *Bush Scholars and Activists* 94
9.2 *The Bush Mode of Production Now* 95
9.3 *Socialism and Feminism Enter the Bush* 96
10 Conclusion 97
11 Source Note 98

5 **Mode of Production and Materialist Cultural Politics** 99
1 Introduction 99
2 Spatial Logics I: Capitalism 102
3 Spatial Logics II: Tributary 105
4 Spatial Logics III: Bush 106
5 Temporal Logics I: Capitalism 108
6 Temporal Logic II: Tributary 110
7 Temporal Logic III: Bush 111
8 The Logic of Subjectivity across Three Modes of Production 113
9 Ways of Knowing 116

10 Conclusion 118
11 Source Note 119

6 Mode of Production Now 120
1 Capitalist Crises and Socialist Possibilities 120
2 There Is No Outside? 126
3 Totality and Totalisation 128
4 Totalisation, Colonialism, and Mode of Production 131
5 The Bifurcated Colonial Subject 133
6 Totalisation in the Capitalist World 135
7 Identities and Modes of Production 136
8 Ecology and the Anthropocene 138
9 Egalitarianism and Affluence: The Socialism to Come 140
10 Source Note 142

References 143
Index 149

Preface

We, Heller and Kulchyski, are scholars and activists working out of a Canadian national context but with an eye to global developments. Heller is a historian and has written extensively on French revolutionary history, but also on the 'transition debate' regarding the origin of capitalism, the nature of the U.S. university as a site of social struggle, and many other issues. Kulchyski was trained in politics and teaches in an Indigenous Studies context; he works on the intersection of history, culture, law and politics in the struggles of bush people for justice, with a special emphasis on the struggles of Inuit, Dene and Ininew (Cree) peoples in the Subarctic and Arctic regions of the Canadian settler colony.

Both of us have also had long engagements as activists. Heller's activist practice has been primarily with working people in anti-capitalist struggles through a variety of venues over the last fifty years. Kulchyski has worked as a union activist fighting for better working conditions for precarious sessional faculty, and in a variety of small social justice groups working on specific struggles for justice of First Nations people (Friends of Stoney Point, Friends of Grassy Narrows, Innu Support Group, and many others), as well as having been a founding member of Defenders of the Land, a national organisation of grass roots land defenders in Canada. Kulchyski is most recently actively involved in Wa Ni Ska Tan (Wake Up!), a research-driven alliance of hydro-affected Indigenous northern communities in Manitoba.

We bring to bear our divergent and overlapping reading trajectories and our embodied involvement in activist struggle on the material we present herein. We attempt to be politically engaged in our scholarly work, and theoretically informed in our commitments to struggle. Our borrowings from both theory and practice have motivated and informed the words that follow.

Peter expresses his love and gratitude to Jessica Jacobson-Konefall for her life changing support and for the many conversations that have fed and continue to feed his thinking; Henry sends love to his partner Laura Soriano who sustains him.

Introduction

This book argues for the urgency of the Marxist concept 'mode of production' to the political challenges posed by the current historical conjunction. We are convinced that revolution, a deep-structural transformation of the constraining logic of our time, is a necessary and urgent task. We argue that the concept mode of production is central to revolutionary thought and action. We also show how the concept, long used as a focal point in understanding struggles of working people, can be drawn upon to think critically about a wide range of political demands that have emerged in the last few decades, from racialised, colonised, gendered and able-ist oppressions to the demands of black, Indigenous, people of colour (BIPOC) and lesbians, gays, bisexual, transexual, queer (LGBTQ) and two-spirited people. We argue that in broad terms the cultural politics that demand interrogation and the ecological crises that demand response can be illuminated in interesting ways when examined through the lens of a materialism that leans in to the questions raised by an analysis grounded in the concept 'mode of production'.

This is not a book of intense, abstract theoretical reflection, though we draw from the Marxist canon, particularly the writings of Marx and Engels, but also Gramsci, the Frankfurt School of critical theory, the work of French structuralists Althusser and Poulantzas, global political economy, including elements of post-colonial theory, and a range of other scholarly and theoretical sources, with the hope of recentring the concept 'mode of production' as a tool of critical social practice. We have tread lightly with our scholarly apparatus, quoting occasionally, referring to specific theorists or scholars somewhat more frequently, and indicating at the end of each chapter the main sources for the arguments presented. We try to show where our view is widely contested and where there is a critical, scholarly or left-political consensus on particular issues as well.

While the concept 'mode of production' was first deployed by Marx and Engels, and remains in wide circulation among materialist thinkers, we think a broad re-statement of this terrain can be enlivened by drawing upon empirical, scholarly and theoretical work developed, particularly over the last fifty years. Hence an aspect of our work here can be seen as a modest reinvigoration of a notion central to Marxist theory. We have observed that where the concept is most used, these days, it is deployed either in the scholarly debates focused on the transition from feudalism to capitalism, or to discuss shifts and periods within the capitalist mode of production. The conflict between modes of production, and the opening afforded by our ability to think towards new modes of production, are also issues of critical relevance in the enormous struggles faced during the current overlapping crises. We are particularly concerned that certain theoretical tendencies that jettison the concept underplay the degree to which their self-proclaimed radicalism actually heralds a rather tepid social democratic accommodation with capital: Wolf's clothing is worn by many theoretical sheep in these days.

Following the near financial collapse of 2008 and the striking failures of Western governments to cope with the COVID-19 pandemic (in which we supposedly learned how much the 'economy' is more important than the lives of people), it became clear to many people that the neo-liberal model of governance was bankrupt. Neo-liberalism was itself a response the rich had developed and promoted to meet the challenge posed by the post-war welfare state-inspired programmes and services that attempted to meet the demands of ordinary people, demands themselves often propelled by the strength of trade union movements at the time.

Neoliberalism made 'taxation' a dirty word: 'Increase taxes' became a phrase banned from public discourse in the 1980s under the influence of Ronald Reagan in the United States and Margaret Thatcher in the United Kingdom. Neo-liberalism represents class warfare: an attack by the wealthy elites and their lackeys on the very notion of a public, of a shared community, of any element of social existence that might place itself above the needs of capital. In the last four decades, in the capitalist centres, states vociferously attacked unions, and successfully advocated for cutbacks to social spending in order to support tax breaks for the wealthy and the corporate world, sparking a considerable increase in inequality: The rich live perhaps more than ever before in a very different world than that of ordinary people, own so much wealth above and beyond any needs they can conceive, that they have taken to flying into outer space in a grand spectacle of how much better they are than anyone else. The capitalist state also remains incapable of coming to grips with global warming and the massive social cost, including in forced immigration, already being seen as one of the real-world impacts of climate change.

While there are still proponents of neoliberalism, the discrediting of the doctrine has turned more people back towards seriously questioning whether capitalism on the whole is all its proponents cheerlead for. And the cheerleaders of capitalism have turned to the more brutal 'populism' of proto- or actual fascist demagoguery to prop up the system that benefits them. In these swirling winds of political conflict, there has been a discernable increase in interest in Marxism as the strongest and most coherent criticism of capitalism. But the neoliberal period also gave rise to a variety of political tendencies associated with different forms of specific marginalisation: race, gender, sexual orientation, ability discrepancies, colonial status, all drawing on their own historical struggles and ideas – specific traditions as oppressed social groups. Thinkers embedded in these 'traditions of the oppressed' developed elaborate theoretical positionings and often also set social subjects against capitalism, as did a growing ecological critique not entirely or exclusively devoted to climate change.

Class conflict is clearly a critical element in the waves and counterwaves of historical change we have seen in the post-war period (and of course earlier). And social class is present in everyday life: We learn at an early age how to recognise the trappings of class; we know what restaurants to go into or not; we learn the subtle difference between those who 'dress down' and those who are down; we desperately attempt to socialise 'upwards' and gain favour from those who present themselves as our 'betters'. The elements of class difference and concomitant social hierarchies are such a deep-seated part of everyday sociality that they are barely perceptible. An effort of will is required to notice, attend to, 'call out' even, the everyday modalities of a nearly all-pervasive elitism endemic to contemporary times. Though we affirm the reality of class conflict, we also note that deep seated social structures around gender, around race, around sexual difference and sameness, around differences of ability, around colonial positioning, all call to the depths of our social and individual being. Newer generations of people are moved and motivated by these struggles and by environmental issues. Although there are of course overlapping social positions, every particularity can develop a philosophy that universalises and centres its specific call to justice. Hence, moving to a broader level of analysis – the level that Marx called mode of production – allows for framing these struggles in a manner that helps to articulate the solidarities central to challenging the variety of hierarchies that intersect in our domination.

In this rapidly evolving historical conjunction, then, we thought a text devoted to a crucial element of Marx's thought, the overarching concept 'mode of production', might be a useful guide for readers interested in Marx as activists or as theorists or as both. This book is designed to appeal to an audience that may have read some Marx, or some recent social theory, or be interested in engaging in such a reading. Much of the ground we will cover involves material that is well-known, though we try to bring recent research to bear and to cover a wide field of reference, from history to anthropology to political theory and cultural studies. We also on occasion get into denser theoretical issues and offer some of our own original ideas.

We approach this material not with a wholescale rejection of what are often called 'identity politics'; there is much to be learned, that must be learned, from the insights of people who are socially marginalised in distinct ways and from those who theorise these marginalisations. A Marxism that cannot learn, that is satisfied to repeat the same formulas, does not live up to the standard Karl Marx set for himself as a thinker, nor to the political challenges we face. We attempt to show how the concept 'mode of production' is a critical aid in thinking through political struggles that are not immediately class-based; and thereby we hope to show how deeper alliances across the left-spectrum can be built.

Marx did accurately describe the structural parameters of the current system: As the philosopher Jean-Paul Sartre once observed, Marxism is the untranscendable philosophy of our era. That means, in identifying the fundamental nature of the current dominant system as based on the necessity for capital to grow (or accumulate), Marxism makes it relatively easy for activists to know what struggles take place within the parameters of the capitalist system as accommodations, and what struggles pose a challenge to the very logic or basis of our political epoch.

Marxism is rich with conceptual insight that allows us to unpack the immediate conjunction of forces and events as well as the possibility of longer-term, deep structural or revolutionary change. Furthermore, and as we argue, the concept 'mode of production' gives us particular purchase on the variety of identities that capitalism has not served well: not only male factory workers, but working women, racialised subjects, queer (LGBTQ2S) subjects, colonised peoples, differently abled peoples, and so on. We write for activists with a theoretical bent, for theorists of the everyday, for any of those social justice activists who have come to see the possibility that Marxism may be a useful or even essential intellectual resource.

To demonstrate the overarching value of the concept 'mode of production' we would briefly like to take note of a recent, quite widely read, study where its salience was not drawn upon. Although a worthy read offering much food for critical thought, the agency or action or practices they advocate or imply are deeply undercut by the deliberate refusal to take on board the intellectual resources Marxism offers. We will here very briefly discuss *The Dawn of Everything* by David Graeber and David Wengrow, although references to it will appear in later chapters as well. The authors are 'radicals' who are deeply unhappy with the status quo and are willing to fight for change: They are on 'the left' broadly speaking. Although the work is not a deep philosophical treatise, it is somewhat accessible to what is called a general audience, and has garnered a good deal of attention.

In *The Dawn of Everything*, Graeber and Wengrow discuss the origins of human society, dismissing the question associated with French Enlightenment philosopher Jean-Jacques Rousseau about 'the origin of inequality' and asserting that agriculture was not a change in productive practice that led to patriarchy, private property and the state (as Engels, following Marx, has it). In order to make the case, they produce a good deal of evidence to show there were hierarchical societies among gathering and hunting peoples, and there were egalitarian cities in the early Neolithic (agricultural) period. There have been a wide variety of grounds for criticism of their claims: They reject the importance of events that happen before the period they look to, they are often fairly fast and loose with the factual basis of their arguments, they consistently skip over discussions that really require careful analysis, and they emphasise human freedom to such an extent that only environmental factors appear to limit the nature of social structure (what is called voluntarism by historical materialists). To these criticisms we would add that they entirely and explicitly dismiss the concept of 'mode of production'.

In a chapter called 'Many Seasons Ago: Why Canadian foragers kept slaves and their Californian neighbours didn't; or, the problem with "modes of production"' they devote a total of two paragraphs to a summary dismissal of the concept. It is worth following their brief argument:

> Classifying these groups according to how much they farmed, fished or hunted tells us little of their actual histories. What really mattered, in terms of the ebb and flow of power and resources, was their use of organized violence to 'feed off' other populations. Sometimes the foraging peoples ... had the upper hand militarily over their agricultural neighbors. ... [T]he idea of classifying human societies by 'modes of subsistence' looks decidedly naïve. How, for instance, would we propose to classify foragers who consume *domestic* crops, exacted as tribute from nearby farming populations? Marxists, who refer to 'modes of production', do sometimes allow for a Tributary Mode, but this has always been linked to the growth of agrarian states and empires. ... What really needs to be theorized here is not just the mode of production practiced by the victims of predation, but also that of the non-producers who prey on them. Now wait. A non-productive mode of production? This sounds like a contradiction in terms. But it's only so if we limit the meaning of production strictly to the creation of food or goods. And maybe we shouldn't.[1]

As frequently happens in the book, though, they remain entirely inconsistent in their application of their own view. They never step aside from describing the societies they examine as 'gatherers' or 'agriculturalists' (terms associated with the core subsistence activities, otherwise known as production). The clas-

1 Graeber and Wengrow 2021, pp. 188–9.

sificatory value of the terms are never in practice dismissed by them and retain centrality in the way they describe different social forms in the period they examine: The terms foraging, hunting, farming and agriculture are among the most prominent in their index and are in our reading always used at some point as a descriptor of every particular social collective they are discussing at any particular point in the text.

Without a concept like mode of production their text slides into the notion that in any historical period humans are capable of creating whatever kind of social relations they want to. Hence, gatherers and hunters or agriculturalists in their view are both as capable of making hierarchical or egalitarian societies (though, apparently, that they are foragers or agriculturalists retains its importance in actual discussions). They don't care to notice that the vast majority of gatherers and hunters are egalitarian, and the evidence for sustained hierarchies among them is actually quite sparse. And the egalitarian cities they describe ultimately disappear into a remarkable set of highly socially stratified, unequal, patriarchal, property-based social forms, which were drawn on to lay a foundation for capitalism. Alex Callinicos, among many other Marxists, emphasises that 'to say that a society has a structure is to say that there are limits to the extent to which it may vary without becoming an instance of a different kind of society'.[2] In contrast to this, Graeber and Wengrow naively (the word they use) present an approach in which, 'hey ho, everything goes' is the main motif. To the extent that on occasion they characterise gatherers and hunters as 'free societies' it may be said that their stated anarchism slides over into toxic libertarianism. By deliberately refusing to think about structural parameters established by the modes of production, parameters which themselves condition the range of actions people can take, their rich, well-written, engaging text in the end offers no help to any of those who are engaged in a serious project of social change. It says, in effect: 'People have always been hierarchical. People have always been egalitarian. It's your choice'. We think understanding what structural changes in the past were consequential and what changes were not, based on the core productive strategies of a social formation, elucidates more rigorous historical thought and opens a politically sharper sense of contemporary political dynamics.

Chapter 1 reviews the place of the concept 'mode of production' in the Marx/Engels canon, examines briefly contemporary Marxist, particularly in the structural tradition, usages of the concept, argues for the Wolfian/Amir notion of three primary modes (gathering and hunting or 'bush' in this account, tribu-

2 Callinicos 2004, p. 38.

tary and capitalist), offers a short review of these modes and makes illustrative allusion to the contemporary value of the term. At this stage we deploy the conventional Marxist notions of relations and forces of production to describe the modes, a description that will be supplemented by discussion of cultural platforms in Chapter 5. Broadly speaking, this analysis draws on the dialectical Marxist tradition recently articulated by Fredric Jameson, though we also employ feminist, queer, decolonial, anti-racist and Indigenous thinking.

Chapter 2 is a historically inflected examination of capitalism, examining the various shifts in capital accumulation strategies, the debates around the origin of capitalism, attempting to provide a balanced perspective on the historical contributions of capitalism while clearly demonstrating the emerging contradictions and dysfunctions attendant on world capitalism. The chapter draws on recent studies that emphasise the global dimensions of capitalist development.

Chapter 3 draws upon the scholarly literature pertaining to the tributary mode of production, by which we include so-called ancient city-state societies of Asia, the Americas, Europe, Africa and the Middle East, as well as the variety of feudalisms that were more recent forms of the fundamental, tributary arrangement underpinning the mode. We also tackle the transition to capitalism from the historical vantage point of the development within tributary based social formations.

Chapter 4 describes the 'bush mode of production', called by Marx primitive communism and by others nomadic foragers or gatherers and hunters. The description rests heavily on anthropological material developed in the last fifty years, often as theoretical support for the struggles of bush people against capitalist totalisation.

These three chapters are organised from capitalism to the bush mode, and so not written to mimic the so-called 'ascent of man', as a way of emphasising that each of the three modes involves advantages and disadvantages to the people who deployed them. That is, by sequencing our discussion from capitalism to the tributary and finally bush mode, we are able to challenge the progressive stage theory that implies in all ways that the latest is an improvement on the last: the narrative of 'every day in every way things get better and better' that underlies mainstream history.

Chapter 5 involves comparing the three modes with specific attention to the way in which each mode actualises a distinct set of 'cultural platforms' which provide a consistent foundation for the expressive culture and everyday life represented within the mode. The principles upon which temporality, spatiality, knowledge and subjectivity are built vary across the modes and are consistent within them. Expressive culture within each mode is constrained by and actively reproduces these platforms. This analysis supplements the more commonly Marxist project of seeing the modes in terms solely of relations and forces of production. While the complex interaction of relations and forces of production are key in thinking about social transformation, we think the interaction is felt or lived in an everyday life level that also deserves interrogation. It is here that the authors argue for a materialist cultural analysis: The cultural platforms are material forces that inflect ways of being in the world.

Chapter 6 points to a number of theoretical and political implications of the apparatus we deploy. In particular, the notion of revolutionary change towards socialism is re-emphasised as a fundamental political objective. The notion that 'there is no outside' of capital or empire or the written is challenged as a coded social-democratic politics that surrenders all hope of meaningful change before the first shot is fired. We strongly question the growing use of the term 'Anthropocene' as a way of displacing the concept mode of production. The chapter also deals specifically with capitalist totalisation as a fulcrum in the relation to the other modes of production. The aim is to draw out a theory of the capitalist state as a third distinct totalising force – along with the accumulation of capital and the expansion of the commodity form – only nascently theorised by Marxism (Gramsci and Poulantzas offer evocative understandings). This allows us to look at so called 'Indigenous struggles' in contemporary times with a stronger materialist vision that draws inspiration from bush peoples' egalitarian social relations, for example. We provide some initial thoughts about how BIPOC, LGBTQ2S, environmental and working-class struggles all gain different inflections and resources when placed in the context of analyses grounded in the concept mode of production.

In a time when fundamental change is urgently required and demanded, we return to the most fundamental of concepts in the Marxist canon. There can be no doubt that cascading crises have exposed ecological and social limits to the rule of capital. Tepid politics and accommodations with capital will not be a sufficient response. We are convinced that a clear-sighted acknowledgement of the problems we all face inexorably forces us to acknowledge that the current political and economic system is entirely unsustainable, that accommodation with the rule of capital has proven to lead to half-hearted measures where they don't actually exacerbate the problem, that technical solutions to global ecological crises cannot be found in the absence of a dramatic social change, that grasping at the nub of the problem forces us to think about what it means when we, socialists, say 'another world is possible'. That other world is a world shaped by a new allocation of resources, a more meaningful and participatory form of democratic decision making, a dramatically different sense of community and ethic of caring and a context of public discussion in which all of these issues can be confronted openly and honestly.

CHAPTER 1

Concerning a Concept

A time, a historical moment, that evokes the real possibility of global catastrophe surely demands an intellectual response that unflinchingly confronts the myriad natural and social forces that have broached the crises. While crises thinking is a prevalent feature of human reality in particular kinds of social moments (the end is always nigh), the last half century has seen the continuing threat of nuclear holocaust, the variety of ecological crises from ozone depletion to species eradication based in large part on habitat devastation, to a world-wide set of energy crises, to the existential threat of global warming that all told suggests apocalypse. Increasing class conflict in the wake of growing economic and social inequality meanwhile, and in the conjoined context of the clear economic policy failures of neoliberalism in 2008 and during the COVID-19 pandemic, has led the ruling bourgeoisie once again to flirt with various pernicious fascist political projects and to war-mongering. For all that our knowledge of millenarian movements in history might temper our concern, it is nevertheless hard to ignore the urgencies of the moment. The single issue of global warming is enough of a problem to confront; and since it is a human-made problem it cannot be confronted without thinking about the kind of society that made and perpetuates and actually continues to aggravate it. Our species, as organised in the dominant social form at this time, capitalism, is destroying its own home at an unprecedented and terrifying rate. Our species has created and encouraged individual types who are blithely unconcerned about the implications of their actions, as long as they continue to enjoy their pampered life spans or personally and individually revel in their plastic pleasures. Our species daily pledges allegiance to a system that is destroying the conditions which allow it to exist. Dramatic change is called for on a global scale and in a short period of time. There is a word for this kind of change – breath it, sing it, whisper it and wave its banner: revolution.

Revolution in the current context means ending the centuries-old dominance of capitalism and melting the iron grip of the logic of capital accumulation over all decision making now engaged by ruling classes and their structures of dominance. In our time revolution means epochal and qualitative change on a world scale. Such a transformation will likely demand a prolonged and complex war of position across the globe. But it might also entail, given the possibility of collapse, the opportune seizure of the system's commanding heights. It won't happen tomorrow, but given the depth of the crisis it could happen sooner rather than later. Revolution in this or that regime will not have a substantial impact on the problems our species faces as long as the dominant social form at this time remains intact. Regime change in a particular state will be merely a step along the way.

But theory demands attentiveness to the structural features underlying the particular global agents and forms that dominate our contemporary moment. The concept mode of production is integral to a fulsome understanding of the structural parameters that work to limit each and every particular regime in power, draws our attention to the broader importance of the struggles of generally marginal 'bush' or gathering and hunting peoples to the project of desired social change, turns attention to the historical patterns involved in transitions between modes of production, provides interesting angles of illumination to a variety of social justice movements and perhaps ushers out attention to issues on the sidelines of the struggle that must be engaged.

Thought at the level of mode of production raises awareness of the limits of the very way of being installed in the pores of a society and the culture presupposed and incarnated in the global, totalising project of capital. And at this level it is possible to critically appreciate which conflicts carry the promise of being enduringly transformative as opposed to those that offer issue or regime-oriented transformations. The latter offer little long-term hope and can, indeed, provide sporadic leases of legitimation to a system profoundly exploitative and incapable of meeting the needs of the vast majority of humanity. Without the concept of mode of production there is no concept of revolution; the concept mode of production broaches the possibility of breaching the boundary of boundaries and democratically transforming the current structures of social hierarchy whether racialised, gendered, heteronormative, colonial, ableist or class-based, and the enfolding of these dominations in the complex articulations and intersections everywhere to be found in everyday life in this increasingly unequal world.

1 An Ancient Trail through the Forest of Thought

An anchor weighs on the revolutionary imagination. The anchor has two prongs. The first is that scarcity is an endemic or essential feature of the human condition. The world is a battle against nature, against scarce resources that cannot fully satisfy everyone. There is not enough. The second is that the affluence that does exist can only be found for a very few, often seen as worthy or deserving, in conditions steeped in social hierarchy. The only ones who can truly escape scarcity are the rich and powerful. It has always been thus, we are told. Hierarchy creates a measure of affluence, albeit for a few. These two prongs have led the revolutionary imagination into an impasse: Sharing the poverty is not the strongest slogan to put on banners. Nor is 'let a new bureaucracy look after you as best it can, while it feeds itself the best cuts of meat'.

We propose a core idea, that egalitarianism and generalised social wealth have been the norm for much of human history, and can be again. In order to do so, we must look past the Enlightenment myth of progress, in which thought remains focused on the supposedly ever improving times and look beyond the imagined, science fiction futures that conceive of utopias based on new technologies that will supposedly surpass want or need. The past and present, it turns out, can be as inspiring as a source of emancipatory thought and practice. Humanity does not need some new gimmick, some fantastic invention, to save itself from scarcity: It has, now, in its possession, all the means to create generalised wealth – an affluence of the many. To get to this, at least in thought, we turn to a foundational concept in Marx and Engels's lexicon, a concept that can borrow from the more than a century and a half of thinking, research and practice allowing for its enrichment: the concept is 'mode of production'.

Culture against hybridity. Identity politics as opposed to class politics as opposed to gender politics as opposed to anti-colonial politics. Redistributive forms of justice versus recognition as a basis of justice. 'There is no outside'. Micropolitics versus challenging the state. Political economy facing off against biopolitics. Utopian desire. Emancipatory visions. The Anthropocene, the Capitalocene. Theory is tied in knots around questions it has made for itself while practice is forced to fall back on ancient assumptions. The 'left' has too often become a vituperative comments thread pointed at itself.

Marx was right: The concept of mode of production remains the foundational theoretical category upon which political analysis must return and must steadfastly rest. Engels was right: The establishment of private property, the state and the patriarchal family were interlinked historical events. What is now called the Neolithic break from gathering and hunting (the bush mode of production) to agricultural cultivation, a process that, it now appears, happened in fits and starts and more than a few reversals of course over perhaps a few thousand years, was as determinant a break to our species as the later more intensively studied transition from feudalism to capitalism. While in acknowledging the elements of progress associated with both of these dramatic transitions, in our rendering we will attempt to stress the ways in which these particular 'revolutions' involve losses as well as gains, particularly in the manner in which social hierarchy gains through them a central role in the social forms they installed.

The concept mode of production, and its implications, remain underdeployed and undertheorised in the contemporary historical conjunction. In fact, it is only in the last half century or so that the possibility of an unclouded and non-ethnocentric understanding of the concept has emerged. While it has been used extensively to understand shifts within capitalism it has not been deployed to understand the boundaries of capitalism (especially in an era when 'there is no outside' has become something of an ethnocentric theoretical doxa), the continuing conflict between capitalism and other modes of production, or the basis of a politics of profound structural transformation (revolution: the mechanism that will lead to generalised affluence).

The notion of 'precapitalist social formations', tribal peoples, Indigenous peoples, are all, for example, terms that elide the ruptural difference between bush people (gatherers and hunters) and farming people. They give no purchase on the very significant different political engagements these dramatically different social forms represent in their conflict with a rapacious and continuing colonial capitalism.

What gets lost in these and similar elisions is a dramatic possibility and, in effect, the only foundation of a way out of the self-destructive morass created over the last few hundred years: It is possible to have affluence and egalitarianism in the same social space. Not only is it possible, but it in fact was the norm for the vast majority of the period of human existence as a distinct species. If today we live in a 'state of exception' that has become regularised, it is because the last few centuries, even the last few millennia, have also represented a state of exception: society organised around structured social hierarchy, concentrated affluence for a few and an attendant chasm of social inequality. This has created an abiding sense that wealth can only exist for a few: Affluence has to concentrate to exist. Poverty is unavoidable, necessary, and a sad result of the fact that society is inevitably an allocation of winners and losers. These nostrums and the whole vast field of ideological and linguistic assumptions that buttress them, and continue to buttress the notion that endless accumulation in a finite world is the only way forward, represent a tissue of lies, told by the wealthy and powerful and by their cheerleaders, courtiers, think tanks, media sycophants, and advertisers for a very long time. Critical thinking also falls into this morass as a whole apparatus of debate devotes itself to grabbing for a small piece of change that may fall to whatever marginal social fragment (and, that is, excepting the poor) can make a claim on exemplary marginality. The biggest prize in moral comeuppance gets awarded to the most marginal. Theory here is the grasping hands of those in the cheap seats as, for their own entertainment, members in the executive suites peel off twenty-dollar bills from their rolls and toss them to the great unwashed.

Similarly, the concept of 'civilisation' and the history of civilisations stands in counterpoint to the broad, materialist historical narrative that emerges from studying the past modes of production and their transitions. The concept of civilisation itself, of course, is an invention of the tributary mode in order to disparage the bush mode, and was a powerful enough ideology that it was an accretion, an element picked up and reinvigorated by the capitalist mode of production. We agree with Walter Benjamin that the treasures of civilisation are also documents of barbarism, and that civilisation, wherever it announces itself, should be viewed with suspicion.

Through the twentieth century, engaged western Marxists invested a variety of socialist experiments as embodied examples of utopian possibility: the Soviet Union; China; Cuba; Sweden; Venezuela; Vietnam; Bolivia; Zimbabwe. The impulse behind these investments was a political strategy that had merit. It is not enough to ruthlessly criticise everything that exists: One needs also to point to or better, embody, an alternative. But the sites of investment proved inadequate to the political weight they had to bear. Though there were and are some aspects of these nations and histories that deserved attention and respect, they had significant failings as well. They also tended to reproduce social hierarchies and structures of hierarchy, though they involved worthy experiments in poverty alleviation. None involved egalitarian social structures in a context of generalised wealth, in part because all were threatened by the dominant capitalist powers.

The human world appears to be further than it ever has been from a notion of generalised affluence and equality. Social hierarchy is everywhere entrenched and assumed to be a ground of the social itself. Inequality rules, as does poverty. Social hierarchy is so entrenched it rarely gets questioned: Most struggles for recognition of this or that social majority or fragment are pointed towards creating 'equal opportunity', in order for some representatives of this or that group to be mixed in with the elites, so that the hierarchy better reflects the overall demographic, maintaining the illusion that each individual with inspiration and perspiration can possibly reach the golden prize of class mobility. It is a discussion that prevents and precludes the possibility of dialogue about class and social hierarchy itself. In fact, the discussion is so impoverished that when 'sexism' and 'racism' moved to the forefront of social movement energies – an important and worthwhile historical moment – radical organisers took to using the awkward and ugly word 'classism' when they remembered to mention the issue, forgetting even the old-fashioned but perfectly valuable, venerable and grammatically correct term 'elitism'.

We turn then, to follow an ancient trail though a forest of thought that grows ever denser: the path of production. As we deploy it here, mode of production is a term used to classify different forms of human societies at the highest level of abstraction. It presumes that how we produce, make or create social materials and conditions determines many other features of social and individual life. In classical Marxism, the two major elements of a mode of production are the relations of production (how people are organised and relate to each other in the field of production) and the forces of production (the tools and means necessary to produce). Within this paradigm, what happens to the surplus production, above and beyond the socially defined needs, is a critical feature that will cast a light on other elements of the society and culture, and for class-based modes in particular, determine the historical dynamic movement of the system as a struggle between classes for power and resources.

Social and cultural differences within distinct modes of production are generated by the mode itself. Each mode of production establishes parameters or platforms – temporality, spatiality, subjectivity, knowledge, and likely language – that act as the structuring features of a culture, delimiting the possibilities of social interaction, the processes of decision making, the form that expressive cultural forms will take (the form of forms). Understanding these is critical to any materialist perspective on culture. Mode of production can also be usefully seen as an expressive totality: Each of its parts/facets reflects or expresses the underlying totalising principles of that structure or its logical parameters within a particular mode of production. The expressive cultures of northern Dene and southern Guarani are quite different, but the values are markedly similar because they are based on the same productive process within markedly different ecological contexts; so too the Qin dynasty and Caesar's Rome as tributary societies or with Japan and Great Britain as capitalist ones. There are differences. They are not insignificant. But they are not as profound or structurally limiting as the underlying foundation of the social form in its mode of production.

2 Mode of Production in the History of Theory

The concept 'mode of production' was a pathway established by Karl Marx and, indeed, can arguably be seen as Marx's most durable and analytically vital insight. He grappled with the concept most strikingly in the famous introduction to his notebooks (*Grundrisse*), in the course of which he debates – with himself – which economic 'moment' is determinative: exchange, distribution, consumption or production. While there are later Marxist thinkers who argue that he underestimates consumption, a view that underwrites certain forms of cultural studies approaches, in his actual deployment of the concept mode of production Marx does not erase the other moments or ignore their critical role, rather he maintains that production, the generative moment, colours each of the others and should be seen as a critical moment within a movement of all the other elements:

> In all forms of society there is one specific kind of production which predominates over the rest, whose relations thus assign rank and influence to the others. It is a general illumination which bathes all the other colours and modifies their particularities. It is a particular ether which determines the specific gravity of every being which has materialized with it.[1]

Similar kinds of reflections can be found through the corpus of Marx's work, even in the very early writings:

> This conception of history thus relies on expounding the real process of production – starting from the material production of life itself – and comprehending the form of intercourse connected with and created by this mode of production, i.e., civil society in its various stages, as the basis of all history; describing it in its action as the state, and also explaining how all the different theoretical products and forms of consciousness, religion, philosophy, morality, etc., etc., arise from it, and tracing the process of their formation from that basis; thus the whole thing can, of course, be depicted in its totality.[2]

For Marx, a mode of production is constituted by two interactive elements, the way in which people organise their relationships with each other and the means, often technologies, they have at hand to deploy in productive endeavours. These are called relations and forces of production, respectively.

Marx from early on believed that the motor of historical change – including the most important form of change of all, the transition from one mode of production to another – was based on the clash between forces of production and social relations. It was the clash between these two which was the source of historical development. But initially Marx gave primacy to the forces of production. In *The German Ideology* (1845–6), for instance,

1 Marx 1973, pp. 106–7.
2 Marx 1846, p. 53.

> The contradiction between the productive forces and the form of intercourse, which, as we saw, has occurred several times in past history, without, however, endangering its basis, necessarily on each occasion burst out in a revolution, taking on at the same time various subsidiary forms, such as all-embracing collisions, collisions of various classes, contradictions of consciousness, battle of ideas, political struggle, etc. From a narrow point of view one may isolate one of these subsidiary forms and consider it as the basis of these revolutions; and this is all the more easy as the individuals who started the revolutions had illusions about their own activity according to their degree of culture and the stage of historical development. Thus all collisions in history have their origin, according to our view, in the contradiction between the productive forces and the form of intercourse.[3]

These relations are called by Marx 'various subsidiary forms' of social intercourse and include all-embracing conflicts and conflicts of different classes, but also contradictions of consciousness, the battle of ideas and political struggles. From a limited perspective, one of these forms has been or can be assumed the source of a given social upheaval. But Marx insists that in practice it is the conflict between these forms and the productive forces which is the ultimate source of such disturbances. Productive forces taken in its widest sense can include social relations and even ideas but have often been understood more narrowly as simply technological innovations.

But this was by no means Marx's last word on the matter. Instead of citing the conflict between the productive forces and the various forms of social interaction as in the above text, in the Preface to *A Contribution to the Critique of Political Economy*, Marx more particularly underscores the conflict between what he refers to as the social relations of production and the productive forces as the source of revolutionary change:

> In the social production of their existence, men inevitably enter into definite relations, which are independent of their will, namely relations of production appropriate to a given stage in the development of their material forces of production. The totality of these relations of production constitutes the economic structure of society, the real foundation, on which arises a legal and political superstructure and to which correspond definite forms of social consciousness. The mode of production of

3 Marx 1846, pp. 74–5.

> material life conditions the general process of social, political and intellectual life. It is not the consciousness of men that determines their existence, but their social existence that determines their consciousness. At a certain stage of development, the material productive forces of society come into conflict with the existing relations of production or – this merely expresses the same thing in legal terms – with the property relations within the framework of which they have operated hitherto. From forms of development of the productive forces these relations turn into their fetters. Then begins an era of social revolution.[4]

The stress here is on the social relation or property relations, which are commonly understood as class relations. On this last point Marxist scholars have disagreed among themselves regarding the importance of the productive relations or class conflict in historical change.

G.A. Cohen insisted that the level of material development determined the character of class relations; class was a dependent variable of the productive forces.[5] On the contrary, speaking of the transition from feudalism to capitalism, Brenner insisted that class relations fixed the limits of the development of the productive forces and ensuing class conflicts were the source of transformative change. But Guy Bois, Chris Harman and Chris Wickham underscored the point that while class conflict is decisive, the strength and cohesion of a class like the peasantry or bourgeoisie depended on the productive forces out of which they were constituted. The relationship between productive forces and class had to be understood in dialectical terms.[6]

Janus Banaji for one denied that social relations could be reduced simply to classes. Harking back to Marx's views in *The German Ideology* he opined that the actual forms of social intercourse were much more complicated.[7] This remark recalls Althusser's conception in which a social formation may be defined as a totality of instances articulated on the basis of a determinate mode of production. The 'instances' are themselves distinct structural levels of social relations and 'practices', each possessing a functional unity and composed of more specific structures. Althusser specifies three instances – economic, political, and ideological – as designating practices necessary to the concept of a social formation. Maurice Godelier takes this a step further, suggesting that the practices of such instances generate symbolic expressions often in fetishised

4 Marx 1976, p. 263.
5 Cohen 2000, p. 134.
6 Heller 2019, p. 63.
7 Banaji 2010, p. 5.

forms which ought to be deciphered in terms of their relationship to the totality of the mode of production. In capitalism, for example, the payment of money wages – a fetishised practice – obscures the real relationship between capital and labour. We will return to these issues both below and in the chapters that follow.

While much that passes for cultural criticism these days emphasises and warns about the transformative nature of various technological inventions, this misses the point that how a technology will be used depends upon the society in which it is embedded. As well as forces and relations of production, a mode of production relies on means of production, which can be specific elements of the forces of production or can be the land base or access to any other element necessary, ideas for example, for production to take place.

A mode of production implies and constitutes other foundational and expressive features of the societies that bear its logic. It implies and helps constitute social agents who define themselves in particular ways, whether as members of collectives or as self-sufficient actors, or more commonly as some balance between these. It implies and helps constitute the form in which time and space are thought and experienced. The logical structure of language, of nominalism, and indeed of knowledge are all embedded in forms conducive to and constituted by the mode of production. In turn, each of these – subjectivity, time, space, language, knowledge – opens venues that allow a mode of production to develop its inner logic. While broad social forms or principles and technological capacity provide the overall limit within which these elements function, they in their own way help give shape to social form and technological development. Temporality and spatiality constitute a form of forms, themselves bounded by the logic demanded in and around production and in turn conditioning the ways in which everyday life, or culture, is expressed, embodied and articulated.

These features of a mode of production – subjectivity, space, time, language, knowledge – have not been adequately theorised within the rubric of historical materialism. Much has been written regarding capitalist forms, and 'pre-capitalist' forms (a term we will jettison); in fact, in recently writing about 'form of life' Agamben appears to want to reinvent the term culture. By in part using this lens we can gain a stronger clarity on the differences and similarities between modes of production, the advances and regressions they involve, and the possibilities they present in the current historical conjunction. And we can see the degree to which these features are naturalised and become inevitabilities within a specific mode rather than the result of social process that can, actually, be understood and controlled by people. This is the key subject of Chapter 5 in this book.

With Engels, and in their mutual classic *The Communist Manifesto,* the theory of class as a motor force of history, a broad description of different modes of production, and a notion of progressive change from one to another leading to an eventual utopian communism, were developed. While this is a foundational text and offers a strong theory of history, it is written from a perspective within capitalist Enlightenment. It exhibits a 'faith' in progress and a self-confidence in modernism that are in our view overstated. We prefer an account in which the different modes do not advance through an established sequence, where each is seen in terms of its advantages and disadvantages, and the very logic of class struggle which inflects two of the major modes is not seen transhistorically, but is rather grounded in each of the modes to which it appertains. We also have a different sense, and ultimately conjoin into one, what Marx and Engels divided into three: the archaic, feudal and Asiatic mode of production. These are issues to which we will return: Chapter 3 deals extensively with this issue, the tributary mode of production. We consistently argue against an evolutionary movement of modes through a stage theory of history, instead seeing each mode as offering advantages and disadvantages. It is of course true that across time there was an expansion of the forces of production and especially through the unfettering of value in the capitalist mode. But this expansion has itself become problematic. We accordingly do not argue for a 'reverse evolution' ('devolution') but given the entrenched nature of self-congratulation endemic to capitalist modernism we do emphasise positive aspects of the tributary and especially the bush mode of production.

While Marx had evocative things to say about what he in the *Grundrisse* called 'forms which precede capitalist production', about hunters and about farmers, his life work was devoted to understanding and naming critical features of the recently emerged mode of production he lived in: capitalism. His masterpiece is a study of two critical totalising elements of capitalism, the expansion of the commodity form and the necessity for capital to accumulate. He also diagnosed exploitation through the production and extraction of surplus labour and the more controversial tendency of the rate of profit to fall. Much of Marx's description and theoretical descriptive tools remain of critical value to us; we write in a spirit of borrowing from and adapting the critical insights and approach that Marx offered. We discuss the specifically totalising element of capitalism in Chapter 6.

Engels, working in part from Marx's also richly evocative *Ethnological Notebooks,* did develop a politically invaluable account of what today we would call the Neolithic break: the transition from hunting and gathering to the agricultural mode of production. Engels's *The Origin of the Family, Private Property and the State* follows the lineaments of the argument made by Jean-Jacques

Rousseau in his treatise 'Discourse on the Origin and Basis of Inequality Among Men' and in our view accurately uses the concept of mode of production to think seriously about the modes of production that precede capitalism. Engels's book is hampered by the state of ethnography in the time it was produced, but captures a key insight that remains fundamental to our account: Social hierarchy comes with the transition from gathering and hunting to agriculture, with the latter demanding and implying bounded property in land, accumulation, inheritance, gender inequality and repressive power.

After the era and work of Marx and Engels, the concept 'mode of production' was widely used in theory and, here and there, in practice. Perhaps the major twentieth-century theoretical account was developed by Louis Althusser and his likewise structurally inflected theoretical ally, Nicos Poulantzas. They rejected the influential model that a mode of production could be seen through the lens of a foundational substructure (that was economic in nature) and a secondary superstructure (of laws and ideas), that had been advanced by Marx in the preface to *A Contribution to the Critique of Political Economy* (1859). Instead, as noted earlier in this Introduction, they tried to think of each mode of production as having a determinant 'moment', with the capitalist mode being determined by, in the last instance, economic logic. They each drew and emphasised a useful distinction between modes of production as intellectual abstractions (or ideal types) and social formations as historically existing societies. This allowed for understanding a particular social formation as involving several distinct modes of production, one that might be dominant, others residual or emergent, operating through specific dynamics: an insight critical to our work. They also, however, had little interest in anthropology and in non-capitalist modes of production. More so even than Marx, their focus was on the dominant mode in contemporary times: capitalism.

Within the sphere of theories of capitalism, Althusser and Poulantzas alike leaned towards what was not prominent in Marx's work, the specific role and position of the capitalist state. To some extent rewriting Gramsci's notion of the balance between coercion and consent needed to achieve social stability (or hegemony), they each saw the state as constituted by a repressive and ideological apparatus. Althusser's richest insight was in how the state reaches into the interiority of individual subjects through what he called 'hailing' or interpellation. Though he neglected to provide or account for how those subjects could offer a range of responses, he did theorise the manner in which ideology and the state play a role in the deepest recesses of subject constitution. Poulantzas's most abiding contribution may have come through his last work, *State, Power, Socialism*, in which, in a chapter on the nation as a capitalist construct, he paid attention to the role of the state in constructing forms of time and space conducive to the accumulation of capital. His theoretical description can be expanded and enriched by application to and comparison with the other modes of production, and through drawing it into a discussion of capitalist totalisation, an approach more dialectical in orientation than either Poulantzas or Althusser were willing to support.

While historians and critical theorists were working with the concept of mode of production as an explanatory lever for understanding how capitalism came to be and how it continues to exist and expand, a separate trajectory of thought in anthropology used the concept vigorously to understand and distinguish between the other two modes of production. Marx, of course, was an avid reader of the anthropology – however weak – produced in his own time and it leant his work a critical purchase in allowing him to understand what had been 'naturalised' and in providing from his earliest writing a kind of moral compass (see his admiration in 1842 for Cuban Indigenous people's understanding of the relative value of human life and gold). While the anthropology of the last century and a half is much richer than what Marx had available to him, many critical theorists including Althusser, Foucault and Agamben, ignore it entirely, to their theoretical peril. Derrida's most interesting insights often emerge from his reading of anthropologically inclined texts: Rousseau, Lévi-Strauss and Mauss, for example. Our efforts involve an attempt to reignite a theoretical-historical analysis with anthropological insight, while placing the latter more firmly with the structure of thought or questioning deployed by the former.

Eric Wolf, a critical figure in United States anthropology, provides the most compelling overview and theoretical schema of the modes of production, while being a foremost student of the agricultural mode. Wolf cuts a Gordian theoretical knot by arguing – against the theoretical proliferation of possible modes of production, and with Marxist scholar Samir Amin – that there have in fact been three modes of production, a hunter-gatherer mode (we will call it a 'bush mode'), a tithe mode (based on agriculture; we will use the parallel term 'tributary mode') and a capitalist mode. *Europe and the People Without History* is a masterwork in part because it synthesises the agricultural based modes of production – archaic, feudal and Asiatic – into one mode. He called it the 'tithe' mode because the mechanism in which social elites extracted surplus or basic wealth from those they dominated, on an everyday level, was through a 'tithe'. Peasants provided lords with labour time or with agricultural goods; lower lords provided military support and part of their wealth to higher lords; cities provided part of their wealth to militarily more powerful 'greater' cities. The whole system was a giant protection racket. And this was as true of mediaeval Europe as of ancient China as of the Incan empire. Notably, Wolf does not suggest that any one mode is superior to another, though he does point out, against the current of much political dreamwork, that most twentieth-century revolutions were to a great extent peasant-based.

Separately, the anthropologists of hunting peoples began to refute the common-sense notion that these represented the most miserable exemplars of the human species. Richard Lee and Marshall Sahlins alike were able to show that hunters constituted an 'original affluent society', to use Sahlins's term. Eleanor Leacock, Lee's sometime collaborator, persuasively argued that the egalitarian social structures of hunting peoples applied to women's position: A gender egalitarianism could be said to operate within the context even of a strictly gendered social division of labour. Leacock's extraordinary insight remains crucial in allowing for patriarchy to be understood as a historical and social form rather than a 'natural' outgrowth or as endemic to our species being.

Ironically, before these theoretical insights could breach the walls of a self-enclosed theoretical palace, the concept of mode of production was jettisoned by a new generation of anthropologists under the influence of post-colonial hybridity theory. Hybridity theory had the distinct advantage, within the academy, of allowing many of its acolytes the luxury of thinking within thinking, unlike the previous generation who had pushed an activist, anthropological advocacy model which itself aided, abetted and allied with a growing Indigenous social resistance in the Americas, South Pacific, Arctic and Australia. Certainly a rigorous questioning of claims to culturally 'pure' traditions worked as a politically invaluable tool to challenge national chauvinist projects. But inasmuch as the project grew, it collapsed under an unsustainable weight of universal application: Particular cultural forms did and do pretend to a degree of authentic traditionalism that buttress patriarchal, class, racial, colonial, ableist and heteronormative hierarchies. However, across the boundaries of distinct modes of production it is possible to find egalitarian traditions that resolutely undermine these forms of hierarchy. A materialist cultural politics emerges from the grounding that the concept of mode of production provides.

One major thinker explicitly denounced the attack on the concept of mode of production, and it is his work that allows us to draw the section to a close. Fredric Jameson's magisterial essay 'On Interpretation' in his book *The Political Unconscious*, involves an attempt to read Althusser's theoretical insights and position them within the dialectical materialist tradition of thought that Althusser himself explicitly rejected: a perilous and genuinely exciting intellectual project. Near the end of the essay, Jameson proposed three concentric, widening circles or horizons of interpretive power in the approach to history. The first is a chronological, event by event, account. The second is an understanding of the events inflected by an appreciation for their role as moments in a struggle between classes. The third, highest horizon of interpretation is that of the transitions within and between distinct modes of production. Though Jameson also explicitly rejects Sahlins's account of gatherers and hunters, and maintains a critical distance from any notion of primordial human utopia, his work is foundational for a contemporary understanding of the urgency of the concept 'mode of production'.

3 Mode of Production in the Contemporary Theoretical Moment

As Indigenous struggles throughout the Americas, the South Pacific and Asia grow in importance in strategic circumstances where capital is seeking access to previously unexploited lands, surely a materialist analysis would be interested in whether the Indigenous resisters are hunters or farmers? Surely such a distinction would be foundational to research and analysis of African struggles? Apparently, the term 'colonialism' can be used to gloss over the substantive cultural distinctions of the colonised, a similar effect of the word 'indigenous', or 'tribal peoples' as used in India. In fact, the wider one reads through anti-colonial literature, even by Marxists, the more apparent that this foundational distinction gets short shrift. This attempt to vitiate the 'colonised subject's' form of precolonial sociality may play a significant role in limiting Marxist anti-colonial practice.

To refer to one example, Fanon was generally a modernist, suspicious of tradition, while another central African thinker, Amílcar Cabral, had a much more favourable sense of traditional culture. The difference is usually thought to be a matter of the intellectual temperament of these critically engaged public intellectuals. But what if the traditions they knew were substantively different? Islamic cultures of Algeria and elsewhere in North Africa were pastoral or agricultural, involved quite rigid social hierarchy, and may therefore have had limited attractions to an Enlightenment-oriented thinker of Fanon's ilk. Sub-Saharan Africa, alternatively, was home to many egalitarian gathering and hunting peoples whose expressive culture could have had more weight in inspiring Cabral (or Nelson Mandela, who also drew inspiration from traditional African culture). Interestingly, Cabral actually uses the term 'bush' quite extensively in his writings, though not to our knowledge the bush mode of production, as we would have it following an Indigenous scholar of Fanon, Glen Coulthard. The terms 'colonised' and 'traditional', like pre-capitalist, tribal or indeed, Indigenous, all gloss or elide this critical difference. It should also be noted, in these times of heightened Islamophobia, that this does not mean an utter dismissal of Islamic culture (surely Ibn Khaldun's *Muqaddimah*, marks an interest in a more objective, less narrative inflected, approach to history?) but rather a substantive engagement with it and a clearer sense of how that culture is substantively and materially distinct from the cultures and spiritualities of bush people.

A summary examination of four pillars of contemporary thought may be useful as a further illustration of the urgency of the concept 'mode of production', particularly as applied to tributary and bush forms, in the present historical conjuncture. The pillars are culture, democracy, identity and possibility.

In the wake of post-colonial theory's critique of claims to cultural 'purity', itself in part as we noted above an admirable response to the rise of various religious fundamentalisms, the notion of cultural hybridity came to occupy a central place in the study of culture. 'Creole' identities, *métissage* and the celebration of cultural mixing came to be the order of the day. While much of value was produced through this line of critical engagement with culture, it came to explicitly reject the notion of modes of production as an analytical tool, thereby in effect also rejecting the possibility of a materialist analysis of the important foundation and typology of culture. It also ignored the fact that the greatest contemporary force for hybridisation of culture is capital itself, particularly processes of commodification. And while some hybrid forms exhibit the subversive quality that Bhabha, for example, ascribes to them, others emerge as collusions with totalising power: Coca-Cola advertisements feature the product as the unchanging mediator across wide expressive cultural difference for example. While insurgent hybrid forms have a particular value in the context of agricultural based, tributary mode of production derived cultural contexts, they may have less critical purchase among gatherers and hunters, or the bush mode of production. And, yes, pretty much all contemporary bush peoples deploy postmodern technologies: What is interesting, indeed fascinating, is how those technologies can take a different resonance in such a remarkably different social context.

Democracy, once a profound basis of hope for the establishment of a power grounded in everyday, working people, has become a hollow shell, reduced to a single gesture: the periodic vote. While democracy itself is almost anathema to tributary societies, it becomes an expression of abstract citizen rights and equalities in capitalist modernity. Bush peoples have the capability of recognising that representative democracy is a certain kind of crime, and instead often continue to activate what can be called meaningful participatory democracies in which each voice is heard. The left has criticised liberal democracy for the creation of a political class and the ability of the wealthy to purchase political favour, the more deeply capital creates a structural limit to the range of choices that can become part of public discourse. There is an even more serious problem: the depoliticisation of the large mass of people, who become democratic canon-fodder. Rancière's quite sensible proposal that political leaders be drawn by lot is unworkable where a population has been intellectually deskilled, but the same proposal would barely raise an eyebrow in bush communities, where every member of the body politic has always maintained their right to speak for themselves.

Identity politics have emerged as a critical litmus test of political theory and practice. Among bush peoples, respect for personal autonomy, the choice of the individual to be who and what they want to be, is a fundamental cultural value. The actual range of individual difference among small hunting 'bands' is a remarkable feature of the bush mode of production wherever it remains in practice. That said, it is notable that in the contemporary historical moment, many bush peoples, under the influence of a dominant culture or religion, have become quite capable of expressing intolerance. The point is that this does not spring from their own material cultural basis and it is the work of the critic to disentangle these intrusions (not to simply announce their hybrid status). Among tributary societies and those today based on that mode, certain forms of intolerance – certainly for religious difference but also along racial, sexual and other lines – reaches something of an apogee. While the religious teachings of the founders almost all exhibit tolerance and acceptance, the institutionalised versions that everywhere carry the message turn with remarkable hostility even on their own members where they may exhibit the slightest doctrinal disagreement. Capitalism, in which in the final analysis abstract labour power is almost all that matters, makes use of lines of difference, from slavery to ethnic differences among workers to gender hierarchy, in different historical and geographical contexts. Civic debates regarding the rights of particular individuals representing differently named and discovered, articulable and recognised, social identities become the fodder of a political system that can thereby avoid naming the one social group that threatens it: the poor. To be clear, it is not that these rights are inconsequential – they certainly are of central importance to those who have been denied them or rendered invisible as citizen agents. But a generalised equalisation of all social agents in the political sphere is a long-term tendential force of capitalism, as long as the equalisation does not spill into the economic sphere, the sphere of sacred private property, the basis of the insulated affluent separate worlds of the new oligarchs.

For much of the twentieth century, socialists invested their hopes in specific 'actually existing' socialist projects. Russia. Cuba. China. Yugoslavia. Venezuela. Sweden, even. Bolivia. All have made rich contributions to putting in practice a better world. And all have made compromises or even engaged in atrocity (usually for political reasons these are more well-known than the many horrific atrocities spawned or perpetrated by the capitalist world). In the post-Berlin wall world, socialists in the west were left bereft of a model. No less astute a thinker than Fredric Jameson turned to science fiction and 'utopian' fiction as a source of inspiration about what kind of world is possible. We agree with him that much in this genre of writing is worthy of critical thought and invests possibilities of utopian hope. But the possibility Jameson explicitly rejects, what could be called an 'anthropological utopia', also deserves critical attention and not a summary rejection. This was Engels's key insight, building on Marx's similarly oriented disposition. We endorse the view, which is needed now more than ever, that in the pores of bush peoples, of bush cultures, there is a grounded, emancipatory and utopian possibility that deserves attention and reflection.

The notion that 'there is no outside' to empire or to capital is ethnocentric oneirism (a useful term of Derrida's). This is a concept that could only come from a self-absorbed European intellectual tower of isolation. Both hunters and farmers retain ties to a different world, to different values, to different material practices – different from each other as well as different from capitalist modernity. A materialist, anti-capitalist, anti-colonial, anti-patriarchal, anti-heteronormative, anti-racist, anti-ableist politics gains the richness of epochal distance in surveying the contemporary moment when it deploys the concept 'mode of production' both inside of and outside of dominant capitalist inflected understandings. In the very least, such an approach denaturalises any of these specific hierarchies (and naturalising them is one of the powerful tools of an ideological structure that justifies hierarchy). Questions around these four topics will be discussed more extensively in our final chapter.

4 Three Modes of Production: Prefatory Description

It is surely by now useful to spend a few words in brief descriptions of the three modes of production that have conditioned human reality: the capitalist, the tithe or tributary, and the bush or gathering and hunting mode. Much of what follows will elaborate these, each will be discussed separately and in detail in Chapters 2, 3 and 4. These initial circumscribed, broad and brief descriptions allow for giving the concept 'mode of production' a degree of traction or purchase on history and on contemporary society. We arrange them in a manner that ensures we do not see a 'progression' between them, but rather a range of differences that sometimes involve improvement and sometimes a debasement in the conditions and quality of life of those humans involved in the change. We do not, by using this arrangement, want to suggest a reverse evolution but rather to, in our presentation, emphasise or even insist upon the contributions made by tributary and, especially, the bush mode of production in the face of systematic ideologically produced disparagements.

The capitalist mode of production is most well-known and most written about, though we will draw out some features that emerge in the comparative light of the other modes. The capitalist mode involves deeply nuanced social hierarchy as well as strongly entrenched social classes. Universities, which pretend to be sites of emancipatory possibility, are a good example, with their presidents, vice presidents, deans, senior administrators, college heads, full professors, department chairs, associate professors, assistant professors, post-doctoral fellows, sessional instructors, graduate students, undergraduate students, secretaries, maintenance workers, janitors. Social hierarchies are also mobilised where they serve the interests of capital production along gender, race, sexual preference, ability and other lines of difference. A very small, enormously affluent class enjoys increasing amounts of privilege and wealth while the vast portion of humanity lives precariously, often in modern forms of debt bondage, in inter- as well as intranational terms. The most important kind of wealth takes an abstract form in the shape of capital. A dynamic process of technological innovation, while at one time seeming to deserve celebration from all political quarters, has come to produce serious threats to the survival of the species. It is therefore likely that the mode of production is only ecologically sustainable on the scale of a few centuries and doubtful that it can survive in its current form for any single millennium. Factory based industrial production, though increasingly organised along globalised zones that differentiate intellectual and manual labour, remains a foundation of the mode. Three totalising forces, the necessity for capital to accumulate, the expansion of the commodity form, and the state, drive the dynamic of change and endless growth and reproduction cycles. Political and economic power are separated: Unlike in tributary societies, the most politically powerful person is not usually the wealthiest. But make no mistake, the state works in the ultimate interest of capital, and the accumulation of capital is its structural precondition. Progress and development are the official ideological foundations. But culture is organised largely along a spectacle logic, and tends towards secularity. Time and space operate on serial principles (the logic of the numerical sequence). Society is increasingly urban, and possessive individualism underwrites a self-oriented and self-interested ethic, though conformity and social docility are widely prevalent. Urbanisation also gives rise to social anonymity and isolation; individuals are not tied to specific localities. Institutions of social assimilation, such as educational facilities, contribute to deskilling individuals of the ability to make judgements, especially in ethical matters. And, everywhere, everyone is or becomes dissatisfied, disillusioned and unhappy, if not actually hungry.

The tributary mode of production, by contrast, is largely rural though usually produces and interacts with urban fortress and market centres; in it we include archaic societies like ancient Rome and Greece, as well as ancient China, Japan, India, as well as Incan, Aztec and Mayan cultures, and, finally, feudal or mediaeval Europe, Asia, and parts of Africa. Social hierarchy is also prevalent, though with somewhat less variety and where the degree of social difference is, for most people and on a daily level, less acute. Wealth is primarily associated with tangible objects, most importantly land. Social class exists, though political and economic elites are here conjoined as a single entity or body: The rich are powerful, the powerful are rich. Slavery and debt bondage are tools used to tie producers to specific rulers or owners. Virulent patriarchy is also prevalent, demanded in some measure by the necessity of passing on private property in a closely structured manner, inheritance being the operative principle. Technology is oriented to agricultural production and distribution; innovations pass relatively slowly to other regions. Culture is dominated by institutional spiritual organisations called religions, and this mode of production gives rise to all the major religious systems that still function: Buddhism, Judaism, Christianity, Islam, Hinduism, Confucianism, Daoism. Cyclical repetition and renewal tend to be a more important intellectual grounding principle than progress or accumulation. Societies tend to be sustainable over millennial scales, though particular dynastic entities rarely last more than a few centuries. Although spectacle logic is deployed, especially by church and state, forms of culture that emphasise communal relations or that ideologically and temporarily overturn hierarchy (as in the famous charivari) also operate, as does a subculture antagonistic to official religious doctrines. Socially, people are community-oriented though a wide range of skills and a degree of self-sufficiency are not uncommon. The ability to make ethical distinctions and have discerning judgement are demanded by the face-to-face social context in which an individual's reputation can be a critical feature conditioning their membership in a community. Individuals are frequently deeply connected to particular locations and home is a central value and concept, as is family lineage. Time and space are organised along the rhythm of agricultural seasons and logistics, with both having therefore an organic quality. Pastoralists can be seen as a nomadic and entirely rural form of the tributary mode of production.

The bush mode of production, also called the 'primitive', 'gatherer and hunter', 'band', or 'foraging' mode, is perhaps the least understood and most sharply distinct from the capitalist mode that dominates contemporary life. The bush mode is rural and nomadic, most commonly involving seasonal use of resources within a more or less roughly defined territory. Bush people tend towards egalitarianism in both broad social relations and in gender relations, although there tends to be a gendered division of labour. Charismatic or particularly gifted individuals could become acknowledged leaders or situational leaders, though this would only be passed on through generations if the same attributes could be found among the offspring. Respect for personal autonomy is a foundational ethical principle. Sharing of essentials, such as food, is generalised. Small group size, bands of thirty to fifty people, was a daily norm, though larger temporary gatherings for celebrations or hunting of larger creatures or herds did take place. Although spiritual systems exist, passed on through oral narratives, individuals develop their own personal approaches, which can vary among generations and regions. Cultural events tend to be participatory rather than operating through spectacle logic. Nomadism decreases the degree of accumulation of material wealth, while productive activity takes relatively little time (compared to both other modes). Hence wealth can be measured in time and social respect, in knowledge and ability, and generalised affluence could frequently be achieved. The bush mode is the most ecologically sustainable society developed, allowing for multiple millennial horizons of history.

While the contemporary world is dominated by capitalist modernity, it is important to stress that there is a tributary or peasant modernity, and a bush or gatherer and hunter modernity. Communal village life and peasant agricultural production are not absent from the world, nor are the values associated with these material preconditions. While all the urban centres have become capitalist in form, significant swaths of rural territory remain village common holdings or subsistence farms, indebted to the tributary mode for their basic operational logics. Sometimes they are able to avail themselves of new technological forms, and the logic of consumption and dominant commodified culture can also have their place; perhaps even on an increasing scale. As we noted earlier, following the work of Eric Wolf, many of the great revolutions of the twentieth century – Mexican, Russian, Chinese, Cuban, Vietnamese – could be characterised as peasant actions. So, it is not as if peasants have not left their mark on contemporary history. Similarly, even smaller numbers of people on even more reduced land bases continue to embody the values and engage in the practices of the bush mode of production. Because they represent embodied egalitarian forms, though their numbers are small the threat they pose is significant. It is possible to always argue that peasants are 'backwards' and need to be 'enlightened' – hence what Spivak refers to as the ideological trope of 'white men saving brown women from brown men': itself a part of the justification for the Afghanistan invasion, for example. Such an argument cannot be posed for bush people, who may exhibit ethical values that surpass those circulating in capitalist modernity. As Marx understood, capitalism everywhere and at all times wants to destroy communities, create 'rootless, rightless' proletarians: a mobile, docile, workforce. This conflict, which has specific dimensions depending upon whether it is engaged with respect to farmers or to hunters, continues to inform global processes of capitalist totalisation. While resistance to capitalism from within has been heavily theorised, the specific form of resistance from the different modes without has been described only through the bludgeon of 'colonialism'. A more nuanced account is demanded.

5 Final Thoughts for a First Chapter

Three concentric circles can be drawn to show the overlaps or similarities and mark the differences between modes of production, as follows:

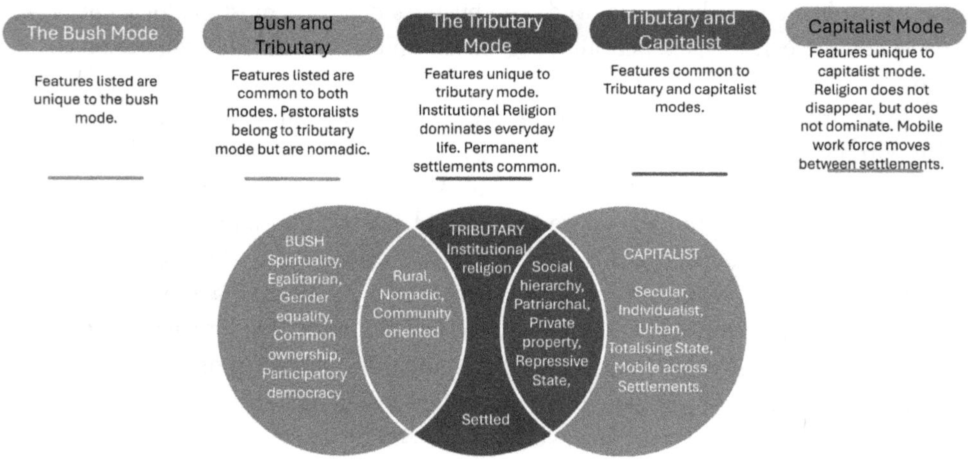

FIGURE 1 Modes of production: overlaps and distinctions

Such a diagram has the merit of pointing out that there are significant similarities between the bush and tributary mode, though many more similarities, especially on the social and political level, between the tributary and capitalist mode which it grew out of. But the tributary mode is not some intermediary space: It is a distinct way of life or mode of production bearing similarities to both the bush and capitalist modes. What carries over from one mode of production to another could be called an accretion: The element, say social hierarchy, is invented in the tributary mode, and is deployed in a changed but still recognisable form by capitalism. Patriarchy is another notable accretion capitalism borrows from the tributary mode. The analysis of these aspects of domination or emancipation is complex because it involves seeing the social form operate perhaps to similar ends in very different contexts. A religion that was partly premised on attacking money lenders morphs in a capitalist context into an evangelical gospel preaching and promoting financial successes.

How does movement take place between one mode of production and another? The existence of agricultural activity among some bush peoples, and of settled villages with a degree of social hierarchy (we think here of Haudenosaunee peoples in the eastern woodlands and villages among diverse Pacific coast nations in the Americas) points to the possibility of slow changes that may have taken place over long periods of time as the most likely form of transition. The ecological contexts and inventiveness no doubt all played a role in what is called the Neolithic break, the transition from Paleolithic hunters to Neolithic farmers. But this break does not take place for all bush peoples, and those who do not turn to agriculture do not thereby become static, unchanging, or 'behind'. They continue to advance on a social and cultural and technological level, developing deeper relationships with and knowledge of their ecological settings, sometimes adapting and absorbing technologies from their farming neighbors. No doubt there are sometimes peaceful trading relationships, and sometimes hostile attempts at land conquest and resistance. The average person has time for her family, herself, her community; she tells stories, she has her own deeply held inner beliefs, she is in charge of her own work, she respects everyone's right to decide for themselves, even her children when she has a few, and she does not hesitate to speak up at gatherings if she has something to say. She has, within herself, the possibility of contentment, or the good life.

Tributary based societies rise and fall according to their own rhythms of expansion, exhaustion, inner and outer conflict. Dynastic histories begin to be recorded of particular family rulers; cities and states rise and fall over multi-century periods. At the base, peasant workers patiently work the land, pay their tithes, and adapt as seasons and ruling powers change, trying to pass on their values and beliefs to the generations that follow. There is constant pressure on producers to pay more rent and taxes to landlords and the state and ongoing resistance to doing so. This engenders a certain historic dynamic to this mode. Disease, famine and warfare recur with enough frequency that the stoicism required to endure them has a social value. There is a deep satisfaction in witnessing a new generation that will carry on the family's ties to a specific area of land. There is worry, work and hope.

Out of the tributary societies in Northern Europe capitalist societies developed. There is much attention to the debate over why this relatively quick transition took place: Was it due to internal social dynamic changes, or the influence of external exploitations on a grand scale? What sort of internal changes were important? What contingencies of the ecological-disaster or plague depopulations proved consequential? Very important was over-exploitation and class struggle in the Late Middle Ages which caused the collapse of the tributary mode in Western Europe and which through various vicissitudes opened a space for rural entrepreneurs exploiting wage labour. But what also makes an impression is the manner in which – in other parts of the world with large populations dispersed over large land masses – dynasties were able to establish a modicum of central control and social peace, as in China and India (which both also saw their share of periods of massive internal warfare). The European warlords were only rarely and ephemerally able to unify their land mass: The degree of conflict led to militarising technologies often brought from the Far East, and then to a degree of technological and social innovation that underwrote massive conquest, producing wealth that could be invested in further innovation. Unrest of working people, changes in land holding structures, systems of accounting that led to the creation of more forms of abstract wealth, increased urbanisation and waves of depopulation and population pressures, perhaps made for a perfect storm unlike anything seen before by human beings. The result was a unique transformation out of the bowels of a geographically specific set of tributary based societies, a mercantile and then industrial capitalism emerged, leading to social sea changes that themselves led to political revolutions and a dramatically new kind of social dynamic. Chapters 2 and 3 provide more nuance to this story.

With capitalism, as with the Neolithic break, the other modes of production do not stop developing. They continue to find new ways of repeating ancient patterns. They trade with and borrow from and fight against the Northern European newcomers; sometimes they adopt and adapt religious forms, or new technologies, or new economic opportunities. Sometimes they are wholly assimilated by these into the new mode of production, which is totalising in nature and so always pressuring for such incorporations, and sometimes they resist, such resistance occasionally reaching to the present moment. While there is no doubt capitalist modernity is the dominant mode of production, a bush modernity and a tithe modernity continue to co-exist: In all three there may be sites or elements of the mode of production to come. How it will come, whether through subtle, unnoticed, long-term social sea changes or through one or a series of social shocks (revolutions) remain to be determined, though the necessity of a such a change is, in our minds, unquestionable if our species is to survive and, eventually, once again thrive.

The chapters that follow describe each of the distinct modes of production in greater detail. Both the tributary and capitalist modes of production have strong historical dynamics and can be described in historical and theoretical terms. The bush mode demands a cultural (anthropological) and theoretical descriptive apparatus. A chasm separates these modes; while there are transitional forms – merchantile capital, partly farming or settled bush people, nomadic pastoralists – the base three modes of production provide an invaluable grasp on the underlying principles of three distinct forms of human life. On an expressive cultural level, there is wide difference within each mode of production; at the level of material culture, values, social organisation, there is a remarkable similarity within each mode. We have sequenced the following chapters from capitalism to the tributary mode to the bush mode as a way of emphasising our view that there is no positive inevitable, evolutionary (or devolutionary) movement, there were only historically significant encounters and conjunctures; though we embrace the concept of expressive totality, we reject the concept of master narrative. Ours is a narrative of radical disjuncture, a theoretical borrowing of Virginia Woolf's blank pages in *To the Lighthouse* that mark the changes, the before and after, brought by war. Yes, there are transitory moments; but in our view these either revert into the mode that produced them or push along a path that settles into a different mode, with all the gains and losses that are implied in the change.

The value of this work, and the compulsion that underwrites our desire to create it, is twofold. In the first instance, it allows for a refocusing of struggle as not against this or that specific class – though this will be a central element of struggle given an elite desire to preserve elite privilege – but for a different way of life. And, by drawing inspiration from the bush mode and from village or pastoral aspects of the tributary mode, we can say that the way of life we demand is both egalitarian and affluent. Since this was once, for a very long period of time, the norm for our species, we maintain that we already have all the technological tools and social experience to demand that world now, not in the science fictional future. Our struggle is for a communist mode of production that merges the social principles of bush peoples and some of the technological innovations of capitalism. The two polar opposite modes can perhaps inspire something new. But there must be room in our world for farming communities, and a rhythm of life based on local agricultural production. Our communism will draw from and embrace elements of all hitherto existing social forms, will pay attention to local ecological context and global ecological impacts, will not be universalising or led by bureaucrats, will transcend national boundaries and will come from forces within and from outside existing dominant forms.

In the second, more modest but equally important instance in this historical moment, we need a reinvigorated concept of mode of production to give a more detailed understanding of colonial struggles in what are called 'Indigenous' contexts: a site of struggle gaining increasing importance and given generally short shrift by contemporary critical thought. In particular, our approach emphasises the importance of bush people, small in number, marginal in territory, but in our view of extraordinary value to the project of our species being and in and of themselves. We write in a Canadian context, where this particular struggle is a key element in the national dynamic. But it is also key through much of the Americas, in the South Pacific, in Asia, in Africa, even in far Northern Europe. Our work proposes a stronger purchase on these struggles through identification of the material underpinnings of the particular resistances of particular colonised social groups.

Among Marx's many insights and theoretical contributions, five stand out. For those involved in cultural politics and critical thought, the theory of the commodity is a critical key; for those involved in activism, the theory of class struggle is central; for those of a philosophical or ethical disposition, the theory of alienation is crucial; and finally for those engaged in political economy, as well as both the theory of the commodity and class struggle, the understanding of capital accumulation as a defining feature of capitalism and the theory of surplus extraction are foundational. Underlying all five is the concept 'mode of production' which is so central to historical materialism because it provides the theoretical context of each of the insights enumerated above. Inasmuch as it also points to the structural parameters and limits of the current, capitalist mode of production, it allows us not just to dream but to think seriously of other, better ways for humans to live. It is the foundation for truly revolutionary thought and practice.

We do well, finally, to remember that Marx's reflection on the concept mode of production in the Introduction to his notebooks, *Grundrisse*, begins with a critique of the notion of society as a collection of individuals. Such a saturated ideological notion underpins, for example, Cormac McCarthy's powerful dystopian novel *The Road*, in which a post-apocalyptic world has each in a war against the other in which the other is reduced to the status of potential food. In fact, if as a species we manage to survive the catastrophes we seem likely to visit upon ourselves, it is only as communities, people engaged in common labour, that we will have any semblance of a chance. Certainly, it is the case that the continued surviving and thriving of both peasant villages and hunting villages are vital to increasing the odds that a human reality may continue on this increasingly ecologically debased planet. It will not be the investment portfolio managers, even those among them who are hobby survivalists with the most expensive gear, who will bear our species through the coming dark age. It is, rather, the communities of self-sufficient, land-based, egalitarian hunters who will make the best scavengers, survivors, and who will present the best opportunities for survival of a future good life. For that matter, if the catastrophe is to be avoided, we best not see these communities as fading in our rear-view mirrors but rather as emerging ahead of us in our dimming last headlight as it reaches out into the gathering darkness.

6 Source Note

We have in general tried to tread lightly on the protocols of scholarly apparatus, referring to the most relevant thinkers and debates in summary ways while avoiding extensive quotation. Each chapter will contain a source note for readers interested in further reading. Our primary sources for the discussion in this chapter come from Karl Marx, especially his Introduction to the *Grundrisse*, his preface to *A Contribution to the Critique of Political Economy*, and his *The German Ideology*, though there is much fertile thought in both *Capital* and *The Communist Manifesto* (with Engels) on the concept 'mode of production'. The References section beginning on page 143 contains full citations for these texts and for all the others mentioned in the chapter and in all the other source notes.

CHAPTER 2

Capitalism

We begin this review of modes of production with capitalism. It is the mode we have lived under for more than for 500 years and under which we continue to live. We start with capitalism because we believe that capitalism is reaching its limits. It is a mode of production which is coming to an end because it is locked into militarism, imperialism and war, insuperable economic contradictions including cataclysmic inequalities, and unfolding ecological disaster: a litany of troubles which by virtue of its own inner dynamic it cannot get past. Whereas earlier in its history capitalism had been able to overcome repeated crises, the buildup of current problems make it unlikely that it can continue to do so. The response to the ongoing pandemic itself shows the utter bankruptcy of capitalist politics: The 'economy' must take precedence over the health and very lives of people. It is producing under-development in some places and over-development in others. Moreover, it has undermined political democracy and lost its political legitimacy in the eyes of most of those who live under it. Its relations of production are in fundamental conflict with its forces of production. Decline of this mode of production is highly probable and might take a catastrophic form. An interregnum is emerging whose outcome – the establishment of socialism or fall into dystopia – is unknown.

We begin our discussion with capitalism because the current crisis of the capitalist mode helps to make the point that understanding humanity's experience of capitalism and other modes of production is important to understanding our past and future. Beginning with the last of the historic modes of production, furthermore, is a way of putting into question the stage-ist approach to modes of production with its rather facile view of inevitable progress and guaranteed happy outcomes. A fall into ruins is not to be ruled out.

The idea of progress, the sunny view of human history, was a product of the Enlightenment and the Industrial Revolution. It was based on the fact that capitalism had developed vast forces of production which potentially could be used to improve human life. It was seen as a final escape from the spectre of scarcity which we have been told haunted pre-capitalist societies. But it is our contention that the ecological regime on which capitalism based itself – cheap energy, food, resources and labour, especially domestic – has turned on itself and is no longer sustainable. Instead of diminishing inequality and poverty, as its apologists promised, it has made these problems far worse. The level of social inequality and poverty has never been greater. Moreover, the further development of the forces of production under capitalism increasingly threatens the environmental foundations of human society. Walter Benjamin in the 1930s presciently wrote that if history is a train, as many imagine, perhaps the best thing we could do is grab the emergency brake.

1 The Capitalist Relation

We will begin with a description of the broad structural features that define capitalism, which develop and expand in a totalising manner through a process of historical development but are present in nascent or fully developed form in the historical moments or periods of the last five hundred years. For Marx and Engels, a defining feature of each mode of production is the manner in which wealth is taken from ordinary working people by elite classes. The capitalist mode of production, which began in the sixteenth century, is built on the exploitation of the labour of workers by capitalists. From start to finish it has been based on the disparity of power and wealth between property owners who take control of the means of production and producers who lose such control, in a continuing struggle. The latter must sell their labour power to capitalists in order to gain their wage or mess of pottage; in fact, in order to live. Radical inequality in this economic sense is the source of capitalism's dynamism and is also an original sin which it has never overcome. This was rationalised as the price necessary to escape from poverty. Instead it promised an expansion of surplus beyond that achieved in the preceding tributary or bush modes, and promoted a myth of inevitable scarcity inherent in previous life-ways as an ideological buttress to its constant self-congratulation.

And capitalism did provide more wealth at least to its primary beneficiaries, i.e., capitalist farmers, merchants, manufacturers, landlords and the emerging territorial state. But historically and globally wages have never risen much above subsistence. Moreover, the apologists for capitalism – drunk on modernity – tended to ignore this inconvenient reality as well as the material achievements of the agriculturalists and hunters and gatherers in previous modes of production. It is also noteworthy that early industrialisation appears to have led to a sharp decrease in standards of living in the industrialising nations, as average heights tended downwards for the generations involved, indicating less nutritious food consumption among common people. Hence the lord – peasant relation of the tributary mode of production was slowly transformed in the capital owner – worker relationship that is at the core of capitalism. While capitalism forces the wage labour relation onto workers, their sense of themselves as a social class has been a key element of worker struggles, as Thompson so vividly demonstrates in his classic study.[1]

Capitalists who own means of production or productive property exploit labour not because they directly coerce producers as do plantation owners in the slave-oriented systems or by extorting rent to access means of production as do landlords in the tributary mode. Capitalists exploit because they appropriate and realise the major part of what the worker produces as capitalist profit while paying workers a mere fraction of the value produced. They do this by buying labour power from workers in order to produce commodities for sale from the means of production, i.e., landed property or factories and mines under their control. Marx measured this in temporal terms: Workers paid a wage make a small proportion of the values they create over the course of a working day. The profit which is realised in the form of capitalist money thus derives from the surplus value contained in commodities. Accumulation of capital or the self-expansion of value which is the keynote of the capitalist mode takes place when profits are repeatedly reinvested back into productive capital, i.e., tools, land, machines, which makes possible the production of yet more commodities for sale and their realisation as money profit.

In order to achieve and regularise this system the whole nature of society must be reconfigured. In capitalism, economic power and political power, while working towards the same ends, become distinct. The wealth and power that had been conjoined in tributary societies (in the persons of kings and emperors) became closely related but separate. Political leaders are not often the most wealthy of citizens and may not even necessarily start off as members of the capitalist class. The state can, within the parameters of capitalism discussed in the next paragraph, even sharply disagree with particular capitalist goals and opinions. Whether authoritarian or so called liberal-democratic, the state is a distinct power centre ultimately working in the system's interest while sometimes challenging particular factions of the capitalist class or engaging in appeasement actions that respond to the threats posed by worker dissent.

The major structural feature of the capitalist mode of production is the necessity of capital to accumulate. There must be growth. Capital itself is a form of abstract wealth. Wealth has become a number, not a pile of things nor even symbolic prestige (which is also somewhat abstract). Although the world is a finite place, capital must continue to grow or the capitalist system enters a recession or depression and is in crises. We like to think of capital

1 Thompson 1968.

as the artificial intelligence that already rules humanity. All decisions made by the state must ultimately allow for, promote, or ensure the accumulation of capital. While states can and do regulate and offer small constraints, any of these is ripped aside the moment capital accumulation on a broad scale is threatened. Hence, during the recent pandemic, the 'economy' (meaning capitalism) became more important than human lives: simply a clearer reflection of what is an everyday ordering of values within capitalism. The necessity for capital to grow is an absolute structural constraint of the established order and, like the artificial intelligences that have created so much anxiety in recent years, blithely gives its human servants their marching orders.

These four features – surplus extraction through the wage relation; the distinction of state and economy, the necessity of capital to accumulate, and the emergence of capitalist and workers as key social classes – underwrite a whole series of other characteristics. Capitalism has been far more urban than previous modes of production. It is centred on industrial production. Since communities of people may have attachments that interfere with capitalist needs, it relies on increasing individualisation and is antithetical to the idea of community. Capitalism has never seen a meaningful place-based community it did not long to destroy. Finally, while some tributary states attempted a degree of homogenisation (see the first Qin Emperor for example), capitalist totalisation is unprecedented in scope and power, with a geographic global reach and a concomitant ideological reach into the interiority of each subject's psyche. We will turn to these latter issues in Chapter 5. We now turn to how these features were created and developed over the past five centuries.

2 Origins and Primitive Accumulation

How did labour power or the capacity of wage earners to work become a commodity for sale? It began in the first place in Western Europe when serfs liberated themselves de facto and de jure from personal bondage at the time of intense crisis as a result of over-exploitation. Peasants and other small producers enjoyed a temporary improvement in their condition. A small number of peasant producers acquired the means to buy or rent agricultural property.

But from the sixteenth century onward the majority of peasant producers gradually lost access to sufficient land or means of production which became the possession of landlords or rich peasants. The loss of access to the land was often a violent and traumatic experience and was sharply contested in massive movements of resistance, though in the end result these were unsuccessful in terms of halting the overall imposition of capitalist relations. Dispossession of subsistence peasants forced more and more of them to sell increasing amounts of labour power to employers for wages. This process is part of what Marx called primitive (original) accumulation because it allowed a certain concentration of wealth but especially because it put in place the social relations which permitted the further accumulation of capital. This transformation unfolded between 1500 and 1800 across the face of Western Europe and especially in England which found itself in the vanguard of capitalist development. Based on the extension of these new social relations commodity production became generalised and more and more producers were forced to sell their labour as a commodity.

3 Value

Insofar as exchange using money and the possession of commodities became the general form of the relation between people, the notion of the equivalence and equality of all kinds of concrete labour or the notion of value gradually asserted itself. Already implicit in the sixteenth century, in the Protestant theologian Martin Luther's concepts of the priesthood of all believers and all labour as a divine calling, a belief in the natural equality of humanity was strongly entrenched in public opinion by the end of the eighteenth century and became a popular prejudice during the French Revolution. Among political economists studying the development of capitalism the equivalence of all kinds of labour crystallised into the concrete abstraction 'value' in the late eighteenth and early nineteenth century, most famously in the thought of Adam Smith and Karl Marx. Purchase of labour power (the capacity to labour) as a commodity sold in the market, measured temporally with the expansion of quantifiable 'clock time', is critical to creating new value. In other words, value is a thing that is both immaterial and objective that developed historically as capitalism gradually blossomed and then came to be conceptualised as such by political economists. Marx in particular saw that it was the expansion of value and of surplus value in particular that was key to the accumulation of capital, an aspect of social life that was revealing itself dramatically in his own lifetime in the form of the Industrial Revolution.

The struggles for legal equality and for customary rights during this same period including the affirmation of the rights of free labor or the legal and unrestricted right to offer one's labour for sale as a market commodity allowed the expansion of value and played an important role in the agenda of the bourgeois revolutions that marked the first part of the nineteenth century. The establishment of the legal freedom of labour meant freedom from the personal dependence on a master characteristic of a slave or a serf and as such marked a real advance in human freedom. Socially and economically it blocked the forcing of the producers back into a relation of direct dependence and forced the capitalist to obtain labour power by buying it in the market in exchange for money. This allowed the transformation of concrete labours into labour power and the latter into self-expanding value or accumulating capital. Meanwhile, for rural peasants, a rear guard action of struggles to defend their communities, life ways, and subsistence strategies fed a legal and political struggle over customary rights that stood in the way of the emerging capitalist need to entirely disenfranchise them.

4 The World Market

As we have seen capitalism started in Western Europe at the beginning of the sixteenth century and gradually found a focus in Holland and England. While capitalist agriculture and manufacture concentrated in these two states the second main feature of capitalism took the form of a world market and developed simultaneously alongside independent wage labour. The expanding or totalising world market was based on the global circulation of gold and silver which allowed both the realisation of surplus value through the capitalist production involving the sale of capitalist manufactures worldwide and the transformation of coerced or non-capitalist surplus production (slavery, serfdom, hunting and gathering) into commodities (sugar, tobacco, wheat, furs) being sold for money. The money form of capital was created largely out of the gold and silver produced in Latin America.

The beginnings of capitalism are hotly debated because, it is thought, if we can know what were the key forces underlying the emergence of capitalism it might help direct efforts in the struggle to end capitalism. Theories of its origins stress either the establishment of capitalist relations of production or the importance of trade. Some insist on its exclusively European or even English origins. Others emphasise its non-European aspects pointing to the importance not only of global trade, the worldwide circulation of money and indeed war, slavery and colonialism in its rise. Another element of this phase of capital's global development was the ability to borrow technological innovations from Africa, Asia and the Americas and integrate these, which included new agricultural products, into the capitalist heartlands. For these reasons we take the view that the development of changes in the social relations of production was most important but that the development of global trade and the circulation of money worldwide were also indispensable. Primitive accumulation within Europe fed accumulation outside of Europe, and primitive accumulation outside of Europe fed European capitalism. It may well be that the confluence of these two historical processes, rather than one or the other, is what led to the capitalism that emerged.

5 Uneven Development

Uneveness is a fundamental characteristic of the capitalist mode. The capitalist world developed unevenly with some places becoming focal points of capitalist production and exchange and others relegated to the margins and dependent on the centre. In a process of uneven development the accumulation of capital in the centre came at the expense of the dependent areas which provided markets for manufactures, cheap food and raw materials based on heavily coerced labour.

In the social formation of the early modern period the capitalist mode predominated economically but the tributary (often extensively relying on slavery) and gathering and hunting (bush) modes co-existed with it and were often linked to it. The development of capitalism tended to concentrate capital in England and Holland while other areas like Eastern Europe, the Mediterranean, including the Ottoman Empire, West Africa and Latin America, became economically subordinate to the states of the Northwest Atlantic seaboard. As a result of and in part in reaction to early capitalist development the tributary mode of production at first became stronger and was entrenched in the Habsburg Empire, Russia, the Ottoman Empire, India and China.

6 Phases of Capitalism

The capitalist mode of production develops historically. The accumulation of capital creates the illusion that history itself is progressive. Marx's theory of historical materialism itself developed out of this awareness and a proper analysis of the capitalist mode requires a historical understanding of it. Of course, Marx never shared a facile belief in the inevitability of historical progress. For him the capitalist mode might well end in ruin. He hoped and worked practically and theoretically for socialism instead. The historical pessimism prevalent today in contrast to the belief in progress of the past suggests the decline of this mode.

The history of the capitalist mode divides into four unequal stages: The longest-lived was merchant capitalism (1500–1780): marked by colonialism and in which the growth of capital was gradual; industrial capitalism (1780–1880):

the period saw the full-scale entry of capital into production and an explosion of industrial growth focused on the main capitalist countries; monopoly capitalism and imperialism (1880–1945): in which capitalism conquered the rest of the world economically and politically; finally, there is late capitalism including consumer capitalism (1945–1980) and neoliberalism (1980–2018). Late capitalism saw a brief period of consumer prosperity in the advanced capitalist countries followed by the onset of crisis and a new and dramatic rise in inequality and poverty worldwide.

7 Merchant Capitalism

In merchant capitalism, capitalist production in agriculture and manufacture tended to be subordinated to merchants. Investment in means of production, although real, was limited. Absolute exploitation in the form of low wages and long hours tended to be more important than relative exploitation or the introduction of new technology and the reorganisation of production in more efficient forms. In other words, in its first centuries the capitalist mode of production did not see any great breakthroughs in growth. Much of the wealth which accumulated into the hands of employers or the bourgeoisie came about as a result of the latter's concentration of control over the means of production or the exploitation of producers in domestic and foreign markets. Productivity only began to rise significantly in the eighteenth century and the advanced capitalist agriculture of Southern England did not exceed the level achieved in the Yangtze Delta of tributary China until the end of that century. Over much of England and the rest of Europe a compromise existed between manufacturing and agriculture in which many industrial producers continued to dwell in the countryside and also produced much of their own subsistence based on family domestic labour. In this set-up the subsumption of labour to capital was incomplete and older means of production simply fell under the control of merchant-entrepreneurs. Meanwhile, over the period the rural and urban population became more and more dependent on wages as a result of primitive accumulation and population growth. In parts of the world peripheral to the emerging capitalist nations, people may have shifted their productive practices, producing somewhat more items for trade or exchange while still often having control over their own subsistence; though brutal and massively destructive wholescale theft was also a feature of the period.

The birth of capitalism at the beginning of the sixteenth century was made possible by the appearance of a new form of the state which facilitated capitalist accumulation. It took the shape of the relatively compact sovereign territorial state in England and France and the collapse of the over-arching political authority of the Pope and Holy Roman Emperor who had hitherto blocked the political aspirations of lesser rulers. The state and the internal market it created provided the political and legal framework for the new capitalist mode of production in the home territory and underwrote regimes of vicious nearly unlimited terror in colonies. Territorial states competing with one another and striving to create national markets with the help of merchant capitalists became a singular and abiding feature of the new capitalist mode. At that time too Western Europe was peripheral to the zones of powerful centralised states in China, India and the Middle East, whose own political and military preoccupations limited the economic ambitions of merchants and manufacturers within their territories.

But the class basis of the early modern territorial state was not merchants but landlords. In England and France it was a reorganised system of feudal domination which made it possible for the landlord class to overcome the late mediaeval crisis in the face of a loss of direct control over the peasantry and urban plebeian population. On the other hand, much of the money and expertise necessary for this salvage operation was provided by the nascent capitalist class which grew up in the interstices or pores of feudalism. It was as a subordinated but aspiring element within the absolutist and feudal state that the bourgeoisie began their ascent to power. Within this early modern social formation, the tributary or feudal mode of exploitation was able to reconsolidate itself based on the support of the agents of the new capitalist mode of production emerging in its midst.

8 State and Church

The early modern territorial state played an indispensable role in facilitating further capitalist development by suppressing internal violence by feudal landlords and popular protesters, helping to create a national market by administrative and legal unification, protecting nascent industries, opening markets by colonialism and war and reinforcing official religious belief. The state at the local and national level oversaw the process of primitive accumulation. The state ever since has constituted an indispensable framework within which capitalist accumulation has been carried on. The state reorganised space homogenously by establishing a more or less uniform administrative grid based on centralised control, subordinating territories and the towns to itself and fixing its borders and frontiers while delimiting its space from that of rivals.

The state would likewise eventually take over the burgeoning expansion of clock and calendar time in their modern forms, a process critical to the eventual expansion of factory production.

Christianity remained the dominant ideology but churches, whether Catholic or Protestant, tended to become subordinated to the state and secularism has expanded as a social possibility. The state used confessional conformity to reinforce its own authority over the minds of subjects. Among other things that the state accomplished was to use direct repression as well as religion as a means of enforcing primitive accumulation and the acceptance of wage labour by dispossessed peasants. Its ideologically coercive power was vital to the expropriation of peasants and their transformation into workers. In the fully capitalist countries of Holland and England, as elsewhere, state churches prevailed but more individualised forms of religion gradually developed.

9 Gender

The gendered division of labour was strongly maintained. It was strengthened by the confessionalisation of religion by the state which reinforced social and ideological conformity. Contrariwise, the establishment of state control of religion greatly reinforced the ideological power of the state over subjects. Suspicion of deviation amid growing social polarisation led in some cases to the outbreak of witch hunts directed mainly against socially vulnerable women. As many as 20,000 witches were executed in the sixteenth and seventeenth century in Central Europe where religious conflict was most intense. At the beginning of the period of merchant capitalism, sexual reproduction was carefully regulated in terms of access to property which remained in the hands of men. Late marriage was the rule and marriage was only possible if one had access to land or a dowry. The upper class had more children than those beneath them. The gradual proletarianisation of the population broke this reproductive system based on property leading to earlier marriage and growing illegitimacy among dispossessed peasants and workers in the eighteenth century. Over time, extended family ties decayed and the nuclear family became the norm among both the working and middle class. The decay of the early modern reproductive cycle and the decline in the frequency of famines and plagues, as well as improvement in medicine and sanitation in the eighteenth century – which we note was good for workers in many respects and clearly a strong contribution of capitalism to ordinary people in its metropolitan nations – led to a rapid increase in the working-class population available to capital for exploitation. Workers in contrast to property holding peasants had many children whose work helped to support the family. Population-increase also created an army of unemployed which kept the price of labour low.

Witchcraft persecutions declined in the eighteenth century as a result of the spread of the ideas of the scientific revolution among the political and social elites. The rejection of tradition and authority as the bases of truth in favour of fact and reason was pioneered by an intellectual avant-garde sprung from the bourgeoisie in Holland, England and France which included the likes of Baruch Spinoza, René Descartes and Isaac Newton. The separation of intellectual and manual labour is also a feature of capitalism, as ideas themselves have become a form of capital in the new technological dynamism associated with the capitalist mode of production.

10 The Politics of Uneven Development

During this period of merchant capitalism, most states on the continent remained feudal and absolutist, but already in England and Holland constitutional government controlled by the bourgeoisie took power through revolutions. The economies of Central, Southern and Eastern Europe alongside those of Latin America became subordinated to those of Holland and England. In these places the exploitation of labour tended to be based not on wage labour but on slavery, serfdom, rent, indenture, peonage and other forms of dependent labour. In fact the intrusion of capitalism into Central and Eastern Europe and Latin America at first strengthened the systems of feudal absolutism and rent extraction. In this early modern social formation the capitalist mode predominated but the tributary (including slavery) and gathering and hunting mode co-existed within it and were progressively transformed by it. Capitalism at the centre shaped the evolution of all the other modes dominated by and subordinated to it.

11 Colonialism

The importance of exchange relations was manifest not only in the gradual unification of markets within the capitalist states but in the growth of overseas markets and through colonialism. Three states – Holland, England and France, the latter an absolutist and feudal state with an important merchant bourgeoisie – vied with one another in overseas trade and colonialism. The most lucrative part of world trade came from the import of spices, tea, silk, porcelain and cotton fabrics from Asia, and sugar, tobacco and rice from the Americas. In Marx's view colonialism – including the production of commodities by slave labour – has to be understood as a form of ongoing primitive accumulation or a means of extracting surplus by coerced and increasingly rationally managed labour and the fixing of the prices of imports and exports by colonial policy rather than as creating wealth by capital accumulation.

Confessional hatred died down in the eighteenth century with the spread of the ideas of the scientific revolution. But religious bigotry was replaced by a pseudo-scientific racism which justified highly profitable slavery and the colonisation of non-European peoples. The whole inter-European and global trade system was based on world money or gold and silver produced in or outright stolen from Latin America. The availability of money was essential not only to trade but also to the developing process of capital accumulation as it was the only way that the cycle of capital accumulation could complete itself and finance its further expansion.

There was a massive contraction of the numbers of tributary and gathering and hunting peoples as killing by European armies and diseases spread by Europeans into the Americas took their toll. The Americas and Africa witnessed brutal devastations on a historically unprecedented scale. The birth pains of capitalism were to an enormous extent carried by the bodies of those who would receive none of its benefits: peasant and hunting families on those two continents, for much of which colonialism remains an ongoing reality. To some extent we now know that the depopulation of Indigenous farmers through the conquest of what became Latin America led to an increase in the numbers of bush people (gatherers and hunters) for a few generations, a process that would eventually itself be reversed but that illustrates the complexities of a one-directional or unilinear historical narrative.

On the other hand, long-term trading relationships developed between bush people who supplied furs and medicines and Western merchants who exchanged them for capitalist manufactures. While absolute exploitation predominated in the period of merchant capitalism there were nonetheless some gains in relative exploitation in the form of printing presses, mechanical screws, ovens and pumps for the extraction of coal and refining of minerals, blast furnaces, water and windmills for the processing of grain, wood, leather, cloth and sugar, shipyards and new sailing ships, and all manner of increasingly sophisticated workshop tools. While most manufacture was carried on in the countryside, there developed an increasing number of centralised urban workshops or proto-factories where an increasing division of labour under capitalist control took place. Ecological damage was manifest in the widespread killing of wildlife, deforestation, over-grazing and soil depletion. As a mode of production, capitalism from the beginning treated nature recklessly as a free good. It continues to do so: Just as it never saw a place-based community it did not want to destroy, it never sees a lightly touched landscape as anything other than a new opportunity for its bulldozers.

12 Resistance

There was continued popular resistance to the state, landlordism, capitalist and colonial exploitation during the period. Revolts against rent increases, enclosures, oppressive taxation, food prices and shortages, religious and cultural oppression, colonial incursions and domination waxed and waned. Pontiac's Rebellion (1763) was the major Indigenous uprising against British colonial policy in North America. During the American Revolution, many Indigenous First Nations joined with the British to resist the encroachments of American settler-colonists. More than a hundred revolts by Indigenous people (both tributary and bush) against Spanish colonialism rippled through the Andes during the eighteenth century, with the uprisings becoming increasingly large-scale, widespread and violent. This so-called age of Andean insurrection culminated in the powerful Rebellion of Túpac Amaru II which swept through the southern Peruvian and Bolivian highlands from 1780 to 1783.

France was unique among feudal absolutist states in the level of class conflict during the period of merchant capitalism. A culture of popular protest developed which was unparalleled elsewhere on the European continent. As the administrative centralisation of the state advanced across the whole country, urban and rural protest became ubiquitous. The periods 1560–1660 and then 1750–89 were particularly disturbed. It was the common people who were becoming increasingly dependent on wage labour and who more and more needed to buy their food in the market. These common people took the lead as the Revolution drew closer. The growing frequency of food riots in the countryside before and during the Revolution signified the emergence of a rural working class which could not grow its own subsistence and had to use their wages to buy food. Notable was the fact that strikes by wage workers, among other forms of popular resistance, also became more salient and were particularly severe during the revolutionary crisis. This also reflects the growing dependency of the population on wages.

13 Revolution

The Revolution of 1789 with its countrywide urban and peasant revolts was the culmination of this mounting unrest. It was mass revolutionary action by the people that allowed the bourgeoisie to take control and legislatively destroy feudalism and the absolutist state. The bourgeoisie meanwhile had developed the forces of production in French society to the point where the relations of production of the Old Regime were burst asunder and it could seize state power in the midst of popular revolution.

The Revolution led by the bourgeoisie inaugurated a new culture of modernity based on individual liberty, constitutional government, equality before the law, separation of church and state, free markets, rational thought and the idea of progress or the conquest of nature and elimination of political and social irrationality over time. Whereas up to 1789 we can say that capitalism in Europe was the economically dominant mode of production in a social formation in which the politically dominant mode was still tributary, the Revolution of 1789 was the turning point which saw the abrupt and violent emergence of a new social formation in which the capitalist mode of production dominated politically and ideologically as well as economically, and the tributary mode was subordinated to it. Revolution henceforth became the focal point of modern politics, with revolutions in the United States and Haiti having preceded and followed the revolution in France. The socialist revolutions in Russia, China and Cuba (and perhaps also in Mexico and Vietnam) in the twentieth century took the French Revolution as a model for a would-be transition to a socialist mode of production.

While the main current of the Revolution carried out a violent transition from feudalism to capitalism and imposed a new dominant ideology of liberalism, socialist and feminist ideas were actively discussed by intellectuals. Anticipating later developments, Gracchus Babeuf led a secret revolutionary group of several hundred workers and radical political activists, who organised a conspiracy to bring about a socialist revolution on behalf of the working class leading up to Babeuf's execution in 1797. In the most radical Parisian neighborhoods, at the height of the Revolution, women were given equal political rights to men. The rights to divorce and female inheritance were granted legal recognition. The equality of men and women was argued for by Olympe de Gouges and Mary Wollstonecraft. The failure of women to advance their cause further was the result of the continued defensiveness of male craftsmen with respect to maintaining the gendered division of labour in the family but also because their fear of competition and the threat of unemployment. Capitalism from the beginning made use of structures of domination that had been developed by the tributary mode, including patriarchal, racial or ethnic, and heteronormative social hierarchies, deepening the division when it was necessary to divide dissent, and stepping back when work force needs or the level of resistance made it necessary to expand the wage labour relation to previously despised potential workers.

Having taken power, the bourgeoisie attempted to deny the common people and workers political and economic rights. It is significant that the Le Chapelier Law (1791) which outlawed strikes and unions nonetheless liberated workers from the conditions of personal dependence that had characterised their legal status under the Old Regime. Based on the constitutionally new guaranteed right of the people to assemble, workers formed unions and called strikes during the revolutionary period despite the prohibitions of the Le Chapelier Law and the recurrent imposition of martial law on them.

During the Revolution there was some centralisation of industrial production and considerable growth in the factory production of textiles and chemicals and the expansion of a factory proletariat. But the redistribution of some church and noble land to peasants slowed if it did not block the process of proletarianization and the development of heavy industry in France until the latter half of the nineteenth century. The overall effect of the Revolution was to provide somewhat greater freedom to French workers while inhibiting industrialisation as compared, for example, to England where the bourgeoisie enjoyed virtually unlimited power. The standard of living of the French population overall improved as a result of the Revolution.

The Revolution in France had also inspired the Haitian Revolution and the abolition of slavery on the island in 1793. This became the prologue to the worldwide abolition of slavery in the nineteenth century amid recognition that free labour was economically and morally superior to unfree labour. Of course, the war reparations Haiti would eventually be forced to pay vitiated its ability to create a socialist alternative.

14 Industrial Revolution and Development of the Working Class

The Revolution in France inspired English workers to try to claim their freedom too. The entire period which coincided with the Industrial Revolution was marked in England by popular riots, formation of illegal political organisations and unions, strikes and political agitation inspired by the French Revolution, English traditions of popular and working-class resistance, and the social upheavals attendant on industrialisation. Despite employer efforts to control workers through the master and servant laws, workers won the fight to enter and leave employment as they chose, to unionise themselves and improve working conditions through collective action. The passage of successive Factory Acts, and in particular the Ten Hours Act of 1847, marked early victories of an increasingly class-conscious proletariat.

It was a fundamental characteristic of the Industrial Revolution that the formal subsumption of labour characteristic of merchant capitalism came to an end as capitalists assumed direct control of the productive process. In response to worker resistance and indiscipline as well as expanding markets and intensified competition, capitalists built factories in which the labour of workers could be more closely controlled and more efficient production could help maintain and enhance profits. Capital entered directly into the production process and transformed it, thereby greatly enlarging the forces of production. Machines powered by coal were used to build new machines as coal mining and iron and steel manufacture replaced textiles as leading industries. A railway boom across Western Europe and the United States created an enormous economic expansion. The Great Reform Act (1832) and the Abolition of the Corn Laws (1846) were major victories for the increasingly wealthy manufacturing class. As a result their social and political influence grew but did not eclipse the power of landlords, bankers and merchants.

15 Free Labour

The economic aspirations of the industrial bourgeoisie were embodied in the notion of free labour. Marx underscored that the capitalists responded to gains by the working class by investing in greater productivity to maintain profits and ensure their control. Indeed, bourgeois political economists argued that free labour was more skilled and easier to lay off than more dependent labour. Workers also supported free labour because it lessened their personal dependence on masters.

This ideology inspired the anti-slavery moment in the United States. It allowed a certain limited truce in the emerging class struggle between labour and capital. It was against this background that Marx developed his all-important concept of surplus value which we discussed earlier. According to Marx, value was the money form of surplus extraction. Its creation was based on the existence of market exchanges between different forms of concrete labour. But this possibility itself depended on a certain level of equality in society in which the sale and purchase of labour was necessary because the supply of dependent labour was restricted. It was this surplus value accumulated in money form which made the overall expansion of capital possible. This expansion of capital was not possible under slavery or serfdom. In other words, surplus value and particularly the expansion of value was only possible under conditions of free labour.

As we have noted, the Industrial Revolution saw a massive expansion of forces of production as capital entered into and transformed the productive process. In the form of increasing amounts of CO_2 in the atmosphere and soil depletion, industrialisation fostered a 'metabolic rift' between the economic development of society and nature which widened into a chasm over the next two centuries and confronts us now as an ecological crisis. It was in this period, nonetheless, that the overcoming of scarcity through growth became the liberal ideological justification of capitalism. It was argued that capitalist growth would eventually trickle down to the mass of the world's population. This has proven to be a chimera.

But in Marx's eyes the purpose of economic growth was not to foster unlimited development but to provide sufficiency on the basis of equality for the mass of humanity. With such sufficiency as a foundation society could limit the amount of labour humans needed to do. Time would become available for democratic discussion and management of the economic and political affairs of the community and the pursuit of leisure activities according to individual choice. The endless pursuit of profit and accumulation of material things as practiced under capitalism was completely contrary to Marx's vision of human society. It was rooted in the idea of political and social democracy as a goal in itself. The more so as capitalism basing itself on the unchecked expansion of the forces of production represented a fundamental threat to the biological foundations of human society.

The period of rapid economic growth and political ferment in the first part of the nineteenth century across Western Europe culminated in the first capitalist depression which helped provoke the revolutions of 1848 and which in turn saw the forces of liberalism, democracy, socialism and nationalism in struggle against feudalism, clericalism and absolutist government across the face of continental Europe. When the smoke cleared, the one insurgent ideology that emerged as victorious was nationalism while the others were at best only partially successful. On the other hand, 1848 did see the worker's revolution in Paris in which the workers for the first time fought for their own interests as a class. Indeed, in 1871 in Paris, workers – however briefly – were able to create a workers' republic based on a form of direct rather than representative democracy.

In the years following 1848, the nation-state – the embodiment of bourgeois rule – which had been pioneered in England, France, Holland and Belgium, became the political model followed by the United States, Canada, Italy, Germany and Japan. The rapid advance of Japan toward capitalism was significant because it demonstrated that capitalism was not unique to Europeans but developed where social and political conditions favoured it.

From the beginning, capitalism had based itself on markets organised by the sovereign state. The process by which the state bureaucratically organised and made homogenous its territories and fixed its frontiers came to completion through the creation of the nation-state. On the one hand, there was a growing individuation of the citizens who were liberated from the ties of personal subjection and extended family, while often losing the ties of community itself. On the other hand, he or she – peasant, worker, bourgeois – was increasingly subject to the physical and ideological control and discipline of the state whose historical myths and traditions were inculcated into the citizen through newly created systems of public education, also created so that in its very form educators would produce the 'docile bodies' required in the productive processes.

16 Monopoly Capitalism

But the dynamic of capitalism tended toward expansion of capital beyond the boundaries of the state into a global market. This contradiction – second only to the problems of the metabolic environmental rift and economic depression – became manifest as capitalism entered into a new stage known as monopoly capitalism and imperialism (1880–1945). The limitations of the home market and the over accumulation of capital gave rise to the second depression (1873–94). In response to these problems, national capitalisms morphed into monopoly capitalism and imperialism. This new phase of capitalism had the following characteristics: a) monopoly control over the heights of the national economies by big banks and corporations which tended to fuse to together; b) partnership of monopoly corporations with the state, which increasingly acted in their interest; expanding export of finance capital seeking ever more profitable returns; d) scramble for colonies or protected zones for investment and markets for manufactures; e) intensified economic, political and military rivalry between European states, the United States and Japan. The forces of production greatly expanded, led by the development of the oil, hydroelectric, chemical, rubber and glass industries. The steamship, bicycle, automobile, truck, telephone and, last but not least, moving pictures opened new vistas for transportation, travel, communication and enjoyment.

The capitalist countries, England, France, Holland, Belgium, Germany, United States, Japan and even Austria-Hungary and Russia became imperialist. Internally, this enabled the economic depression of 1873–94 to be overcome and class struggle to be mitigated in Western Europe and the United States by allowing the wages of the working class to increase and by conceding the legal right of workers to unions, pensions and the vote. The late nineteenth century saw an enormous increase in fixed capital and the spread of public education, the beginnings of the welfare state and the decline in the birth rate among the working class as a result of contraception. These concessions were won by an increasingly organised working class but also because at that time advanced capitalism required a better educated and healthier work force. This marked the first improvement in the condition of the mass of the population in the advanced capitalist countries since the sixteenth century.

In the states which were still governed by the tributary mode – the Ottoman, Persian, Russian and Chinese Empires – the incursion of capitalist imperialism prepared the way for their collapse at the beginning of the twentieth century. The tributary mode largely waned and the bush mode retreated to the margins of the globe, though everywhere, as in early modern Europe, people fought back often under the banner of customary or now Indigenous rights. In the meantime, colonialism and imperialism reduced Latin America, Africa and Asia to wholescale economic and political dependence. They became completely tied to the development of the capitalist West, and their traditional industries and agriculture as well as culture were undermined. While there was some improvement in the condition of the working class in the advanced capitalist countries, the growing populations of the rest of the world were plunged into profound poverty and indeed often starvations or severe famine events from which they have not emerged. The power of Western imperialism and colonialism was reinforced by an ideology of extreme nationalism and white racism.

17 Revolution in Russia

Heightening imperialist rivalry and internal economic contradictions unleashed a period of great wars and economic depression (1914–45). The pressures of war and class conflict led to a successful socialist revolution in the weakest capitalist state, Russia, and a near revolution in the most developed capitalist state in Europe, Germany (1918–23). Russia and its immense territories henceforth developed a distorted form of socialist state which successfully modernised itself accompanied by the mass mobilisation of labour and political repression under the control of Joseph Stalin (1924–53). On the other hand, as a result of counter-revolutionary pressure from Britain, France, United States and Germany, the Soviet Union's development was constrained within the traditional nation-state framework and developed its own internal contradictions.

18 Actually Existing Socialism

From 1917 until today, the true nature of the socialism of the Soviet Union and other actually existing socialist states have perplexed Marxists.[2] Many different theories have been advanced. And whereas in the past this debate focused around the Soviet Union, today discussion focuses around China. Is China socialist? That is the question of the day.

Marx and Lenin believed that socialism necessarily entailed full political and economic democracy and it is clear that both the Soviet Union and Communist China fall far short of that. To be sure, Lenin in the immediate aftermath of the Revolution asserted that the new state, the Soviet Union, was not socialist but merely state capitalist under the dictatorship of the proletariat. His hope was that under the guidance of the Bolshevik Party and in the context of world revolution the Soviet Union would pass through a period of proletarian dictatorship and evolve into a full-fledged democracy. But this was not to be as the world revolution was delayed. Over time, the Bolshevik Party as well as the Chinese Communist Party hardened into a ruling bureaucratic elite which far from declining became self-reproducing and permanent, or so it seems.

As noted there have been many theories on the left which have attempted to account for this. Among the most systematic and deepest critiques of actually existing socialism is that of István Mészáros in his *Beyond Capital: Toward a Theory of Transition* (1995). For Mészáros, the crucial issue is the logic of capital. The rule of capital, for Mészáros, means the dominance of capital over labour which permits the systematic accumulation of surplus labour. The capitalist system in general is thus a system based fundamentally on the alienation of labour, rooted in the systematic expropriation of human powers and the estrangement of human needs. A revolution that overcomes some of the main institutional forms of capitalism, including the private ownership of the means of production and the nexus of state and market, is incomplete, insofar as it does not supersede the capital relation itself. It thus continues to operate according to the fundamental logic of the capital system, even if property has been socialised and the state is given sole command of the society as in the Soviet Union. In the Soviet Union, the state remained in charge, standing in for private and individual capitalists. The Bolshevik Revolution was thus only partial and ultimately self-contradictory. In Mészáros's terms, the October Revolution of 1917 overthrew capitalism without going on to dislodge capital or the capital relation. Labour remained proletarianised. Soviet-style

2 Van den Linden and Marcel 1975.

post-revolutionary society retained a close affinity with classic forms of capitalism and eventually was reabsorbed by them. The implication of this is that Lenin and those who followed him were too sanguine about the dictatorship of the proletariat turning into a real socialist society.

Mészáros fundamentally believed that overthrowing capitalism and vesting the means of production in the hands of the state cannot put an end to capital as the history of the Soviet Union and presumably of China under Leninism demonstrates. The problem is that Mészáros advances this view without bringing it in relation to the history of imperialism, which, as Lenin put it, was the highest stage of capitalism. The states which dominate this global system are imperialist states. Imperialism is a world system based on the existence of a complex of these rival states who dominate the global economy and have imposed wars and backwardness on Russia, China and the Global South. One cannot discuss capitalism or capital without understanding its relation to imperialism. Actually existing socialism, with the persistence of authoritarian government, Stalinist communist parties and hierarchical work relationships, has been a product of the fight against the ongoing economic, political and military aggression of imperialism which still dominates the world economy. The imposition of War Communism, the failure of the Workers' Opposition and the Stalinisation of the Bolshevik Party in the immediate aftermath of the Russian Revolution were paradigmatic in this regard. As Mészáros underscored, the Bolsheviks did abolish capitalism but not capital. But the very possibility of being able to abolish the capital relation itself depends on success or not in defeating imperialism. The last hundred years have seen an international class war whose revolutionary highlights have been the Chinese, Cuban and Vietnamese Revolutions. Imperialism has responded with fascism, war and neoliberalism. One cannot guarantee that in the aftermath of the defeat of imperialism the end of capital along with the demise of capitalism will happen. Without such a defeat of imperialism, putting an end to capital is impossible.

There are those who will argue that the Soviet Union was imperialist. The Soviet economy, however, was largely self-sufficient and surpluses that were exported from the centre to the periphery of its more or less closed economic system mean this view cannot be taken seriously.

The case of China is different. It is by now the largest trading country in the world with enormous holdings of U.S. foreign debt. Moreover, China has developed an exploitative relationship with many countries in the Global South. But it continues to transfer a greater amount of surplus value to the core countries in the capitalist world system than it receives from the periphery. China is accordingly best characterised as a semi-peripheral country in the capitalist world system. Under present conditions, its enormous population makes it ecologically impossible for it to raise its GDP per capita to the level of the core imperialist countries.[3]

But is China socialist? The concept of social formation with the co-existence of different modes within it helps to throw light on this question. China is a social formation in which the state, the Communist Party, banks and corporations in the public sector continue to dominate a strong capitalist sector, which the public sector helped to develop. The capitalist sector mainly operates in the realm of consumption, while the productive sector and finance are in public hands.

The capital relation in Mészáros's sense is still in place but the property laws inhibit the operation of private capital. Within this set-up, a class war fought out at the level of big capital and the Communist Party is ongoing, with the Communist Party in the ascendancy. The hostility of U.S. imperialism is strengthening Chinese socialism. Whether China will be socialist or capitalist is an open question yet to be fully determined. It seems that under the leadership of Xi Jinping the socialist side is winning but it is impossible to predict the outcome.

19 Fascism and War

The Russian Revolution intensified inter-imperialist rivalry and the onset of a third, even more serious depression (1929–39) led to major crises in the capitalist states. In states where liberalism and political democracy were weak, such as Italy, Japan, Germany and in Southern and Eastern Europe, fascist dictatorships supported by landlords, the church and the bourgeoisie took power. Based around mass mobilisation, nationalist xenophobia and extra-parliamentary and extra-legal rule, these regimes preserved the existing property relations while mobilising the population for war. In a more positive vein, women achieved full political and legal, if not economic, rights while the welfare state made significant progress in France and the United States. Welfare benefits also were extended in fascist countries like Germany and Italy.

The build-up of international tensions led to World War II, the result of which was the collapse of all of the capitalist states except the United States which emerged as the hegemon over the capitalist world. The war led to the

3 Li 2021.

victory of the Soviet state and of a new communist government in China (1949) removing most of Eurasia from capitalist control. In the aftermath of the war, rising nationalisms and liberation struggles in the Global South allowed most under-developed countries to achieve political, if not economic, independence from the West.

20 U.S. Hegemony and the Cold War

In the aftermath of World War II, the United States – the last hope of capitalism – assumed leadership over the Late Capitalist phase in the history of capitalism. Monopoly capitalism and imperialism were reinforced. The capitalist mode was stabilised by organising global resistance to communism, liberalisation of world trade, sharp improvements in productivity, the regulated welfare state, mass consumerism based on debt, and intensified exploitation of underdeveloped countries (1945–80). In the United States, class compromise, militarism and perpetual war preparation became an ideological, social and economic alternative to socialism.

On this foundation there was a massive increase in the forces of production and improvement in the standard of living in the advanced capitalist states. Urbanisation, super-highways, suburbanisation, shopping malls, plastics and consumer electronics, and the emergence of mass higher education signaled modernity. At the same time, there was an increasingly serious questioning of the gendered division of labour and family and decline in the birth rate, which put into doubt traditional sex and gender roles.

Imperialism blocked the way forward of the states of the Global South. Indeed, the prosperity of the advanced capitalist countries was partly based on it. Moreover, consumer capitalism had its own internal contradictions. As a result, there was an outburst of worldwide class struggle as well as anti-imperialist struggle in the underdeveloped Global South, highlighted by the Cuban and Vietnamese revolutions, and a growing squeeze on profits which by the 1970s undermined post-war stability.

21 Neoliberalism

But the ideological and political split between the Soviet Union and China, starting in the 1960s, undermined the unity of the anti-capitalist and anti-imperialist camp, and indeed put into question the whole conception of socialist development based on centralised and planned national economies. Internationally, the United States was able to organise a counter-offensive (1980–2008) which suppressed anti-imperialist movements in the Global South, contributed to the overthrow of socialism in the Soviet Union, and allowed the capitalist class to launch a worldwide attack on the working class. The economic aspect of this offensive became known as 'neoliberalism' which is the phase of capitalism under which we live at present. State control over markets was undermined by deregulation, the freer global movement of goods, and especially finance capital, and a serious attack on the wages and the social welfare provision of workers.

Urbanisation and mass migration from the countryside to the cities and from the Global South to the North accelerated. An enormous transfer of wealth from the bottom and middle to the top of society took place, and inequality worldwide greatly increased. The division of labour in production became truly global and there was a gigantic migration of industrial production to the Global South at the expense of jobs in the advanced capitalist countries. The development of IT and global just-in-time value chains created a more or less full integration of the world economy. Despite these measures which saw some further increase in productivity, profit and growth rates during this period failed to recover to those of the immediate post-war decades. Such profits have largely come from financial speculation, an increase in absolute exploitation worldwide in the form of lower wages, and an increase in the turnover times of capital based on improved communications and transport. Wages stagnated in the First World as well as in the Global South. According to Samir Amin, the Global North continued to extract a global rent from the countries of the Global South based on financial and political domination as in the past.

Deregulation allowed the growth of debt and speculative bubbles amid growing instability. The period of neoliberalism saw an unprecedented expansion of the interconnected networks of financial capital across the globe. The buildup of CO_2 which started in the Industrial Revolution began to have serious effects with growing temperature extremes, storms, droughts, floods and rising tidal waters. In 2008, a fourth depression broke out, putting the capitalist mode of production in question. In this depression, the internal contradictions of the system expressed themselves in stagnant profits, lack of productive investment, falling productivity and demand, inability to transcend the state form, environmental problems, and growing popular alienation from capitalism and its economic and political leaders.

Since gains in productivity were central to the success of industrial capitalism, failing improvements in relative exploitation appears as a major contradiction. But the gains in relative exploitation marked by automation, such as they are, represent an additional contradiction, as the constant expulsion of labour from the production process is creating growing difficulty in generating surplus value and also tends to suppress consumer demand. Inter-imperialist rivalries have intensified, with the United States trying to hold onto its global hegemony while challenged by Russia, the EU and especially China. China and Russia have inaugurated a gigantic infrastructure project – the so-called New Silk Road (Belt and Road Initiative) – which threatens to shift the axis of the global economy from the United States and its allies to Eurasia. Meanwhile the United States has veered toward economic protectionism. The possibility of a new world war cannot be ruled out.

The capitalist mode of production has proved highly resilient – flexible within the key structural parameters noted above, and adaptive – over the historically short term of a few centuries. Based on massive and increasing social and political inequality it has been capable of developing forces of production on a gigantic scale. Faced with repeated economic depressions it has been able to overcome these crises by instituting various forms of representative democracy, economic restructuring and consumerism, but also through wars, fascism and imperialism. The legitimacy of capitalism since the nineteenth century has been premised on its capacity to deliver material abundance in the form of consumerism. It provided this in the advanced capitalist countries between 1870 and 1970. At the same time, there was little or no improvement in the standard of living of workers and peasants in the Global South. Since the 1970s, the living standards of the mass of the population worldwide have deteriorated. It seems clear that the promise of material prosperity under capitalism for the great majority worldwide is fading. Indeed, growing economic insecurity and the deterioration of the conditions of life is destabilising the existing political and social system globally. Over-accumulation has become a serious environmental problem. Moreover, the number of barriers that capitalism faces in its effort to renew itself is daunting. We are left with an increasingly dysfunctional system based on stark inequality whose future seems in doubt. Gigantic forces of production are in conflict with capitalist relations of production, including rival states and nationalisms.

In conclusion though, we must reiterate the historicity of capitalism. Capitalism emerged out of the tributary mode of production. It is a deeply historical mode in that capital itself takes a historical form through its development. Moreover, it is the mode that is an indispensable prerequisite to the onset of the socialist mode of production. It is capitalism which develops and concentrates the forces of production necessary to the development of socialism.

22 Source Note

On understanding the transition from the feudal to capitalist mode of production the works of Maurice Dobb, Robert Brenner and Immanuel Wallerstein are essential. But of the three only Wallerstein's text grasps capitalism as a world system. In addition to Wallerstein, Leften Stavrianos, Giovanni Arrighi, Amiya Kumar Bagchi, Alexander Anievas and Kerem Nisancioglu and Keith Pomeranz taken together allow us a properly global view of the history of capitalism. Christopher Hill and Brian Manning supply an empirically rich analysis of the English Revolution, while Heller and Sewell are essential to a comprehension of the French Revolution. C.L.R. James is still the classic account of the Haitian Revolution as is E.P. Thompson of the emergence of the working class. The role of money in the history of capitalism needs to be better understood but is discussed by Arrighi, Mary Poovey and David Harvey.

CHAPTER 3

The Tributary Mode of Production and Capitalism

Having dealt with the capitalist mode of production let us look at the tributary mode out of which it grew. The tributary mode was based on the extraction of surplus from agrarian producers by landlords, religious, military and political elites. Marx conceived of as many as eight modes of production: hunting and gathering, Asiatic, slavery, Slavonic, Germanic, feudal, petty commodity, capitalist and socialist. Samir Amin and Eric Wolf consolidated many of these modes – Asiatic, slavery, Slavonic, Germanic, feudal – into a single tributary mode. Its extent over time and space encompasses a large part of conventionally written history.

Amin and Wolf define the tributary mode as one entailing the co-existence of village communities and a military and political elite which extracts surplus from the latter by exacting tribute. The tributary mode of production is the dominant, most common and most general form characterising pre-capitalist class formations in the last six to ten thousand years, during and after what is called the 'neolithic break' from the bush mode of production. In this mode, there is the production of significant agricultural surpluses by peasant producers, developed unproductive activities, especially warfare, by a ruling class proportionate to these surpluses, and the consolidation of a state structure on top of these economic and social foundations. In his earlier work, Amin distinguished between early and later varieties of the tributary form, which includes the European feudal mode of production in which the village community loses the eminent domain of the land to the benefit of the feudal lords, the community persisting as a community of families. Later on, in the 1980s, Amin reversed himself claiming that in fact European feudalism was not a more advanced form of the tributary mode of production, but rather an undeveloped form of it, 'marked by feudal fragmentation and a dispersal of power'. Amin explains, 'the primitive feudal form evolves gradually towards the advanced tributary form' with the level of development determined by the concentration of 'power', expressed ideologically in the form of a state religion.[1] According to Wolf, what therefore distinguishes the tributary from the capitalist mode of production is that under the former the surplus is taken by force – or the strong presence of force – as opposed to exchange. Force is applied by a variety of

1 Amin 1974, pp. 57–8.

forms of state, which are the major sites or concentrations of economic wealth, though organised clergy and a merchant class also amassed and hoarded riches.

Wolf then goes on to hypothesise two different 'polar situations' for the tributary mode: 'one in which power is concentrated strongly in the hands of a ruling elite standing at the apex of the power system; and another in which power is held largely by local overlords and the rule at the apex is fragile and weak. These two situations define a continuum of power distributions'.[2] 'Power system' is not defined, but the way it is used suggests that Wolf here means state, or political power, which within this system can be conjoined with personal power. Wolf continues:

> In broad terms, the two situations we have depicted correspond to the Marxian concepts of the 'Asiatic mode of production' and the 'feudal mode of production'. These are usually treated as enduring and unchanging opposites. One term is usually ascribed to Europe, the other to Asia. The preceding exposition should make clear, however, that we are dealing rather with variable outcomes of the competition between classes of non-producers for power at the top.[3]

And we note or emphasise that the tributary form existed in pre-Columbian America and in Africa as well.

Amin's link between the feudal and tributary modes is therefore retained and the apparent differences between the two are explained as the result of 'a continuum of power relations', seemingly at the level of the state, arising from the success of one wing of the same ruling class over the other, or even one wing of the state over the other, depending on one's interpretation of 'competition between nonproducers for power at the top'.

The basic features of the tributary mode of production, then, are that surpluses are extracted through the use or threat of force; production itself is focused on agricultural practices including animal husbandry; entrenched social hierarchies get established, including the emergence of contesting peasant and landlord/aristocratic classes; state power and economic wealth are largely conjoined; ideology through the establishment of organised religions plays a significant role in the maintenance of social order.

2 Wolf 1982, p. 80.
3 Wolf 1982, p. 81.

1 The Tributary Mode and Capitalism

At the inception of capitalism in sixteenth-century England, the Netherlands, and elsewhere on the European continent, the tributary mode, which had been predominant for millennia, still dominated. Capitalism initially emerged under the protection of the tributary mode in newly emerging absolutist states like Valois France and Tudor England. At the same time, its development – money and taxation, trade and industry – actually reinforced the tributary mode, at least in the sixteenth century, not only in an increasingly centralised state like France, but also across most of continental Europe. Social formations – to use Louis Althusser's conception – like the royal state in England in the Tudor and Stuart period and the absolutist state in France under the Old Regime were dominated by the tributary mode, with capitalism co-existing as a subordinate mode. Versions of this took place in other polities: China during the Song dynasty (960–1279) had developed versions of joint stock companies, included heavy industries (iron production) and a massive South Sea trade network. Meanwhile, the development of capitalism in the West strongly reinforced the tributary mode in Italy, Austria, the German states, Poland, Hungary and Russia, as their economies dominated by landlords profited from exporting food surpluses to the capitalist West – food produced by the coerced labour of peasants. Flows of gold and silver from the New World initiated capitalist accumulation in the West while boosting the tributary mode in the Ottoman Middle East, Mughal India and Ming China. The tributary mode consolidated itself – sometimes replacing earlier Indigenous tributary systems – in the Spanish colonial empire in Latin America, in which millions of peasant farmers paid rents and taxes to creole landlords and a civil, clerical and military bureaucracy dominated mainly by Spaniards. Likewise, the slave kingdoms that developed in West Africa as a result of the Atlantic slave trade based themselves on the labour of both African peasants and slaves.

The further development of the capitalist mode ultimately eroded the tributary mode. French and British economic and military power came to dominate the Ottoman Empire by the eighteenth century. The attempt to centralise religious and political power in the hands of the Mughal Emperor (Aurangzeb) led to the fracturing of the Empire at the beginning of the eighteenth century, opening the way to the conquest of India by the increasing military and financial power of the British East India Company. The combination of Indian opium (was Queen Victoria history's largest illegal drug pusher?) and British textiles similarly undermined the power of the Qing Emperors in China in the first part of the nineteenth century. The tributary mode was further undermined in Central and Eastern Europe in the course of the development of capitalism in the nineteenth century.

2 Neolithic Inheritances

The tributary mode has been the most common, long-lived and general mode in the long epoch of class society dating from the end of the Bronze Age. In this mode, social labour was mobilised and committed to the transformation of nature primarily through the exercise of power and domination by the ruling apparatus made up of a state elite or economic class. Surplus was collected in the form of taxes or rent from the village community of peasant producers organised on the basis of a gendered (and extended) family division of labour. The deployment of social labour is therefore a function of the locus of political power, it will differ as the locus of political power shifts as between the state and the landlords.

Historically, this mode has existed since the fourth millennium B.C. and has been found in both European and non-European societies as diverse as the *Ancien Régime* in France, imperial Rome, the Aztec empire, and both imperial China and the periods between empires. This mode is characterised not only by peasant agriculture but by the existence of towns, palaces and state apparatuses, temples of worship, markets, irrigation systems, canals and roads. In a mature tributary state, such as Qing China or the Ancien Régime, the forces of production were highly developed. The economy of eighteenth-century France or Qing China were serious rivals to capitalist Britain.

Insofar as this mode took the form of classes, it necessarily implied class struggle. Relations between classes are inherently antagonistic based on conflicting relations to the means of production. Until the Industrial Revolution land was the primary means of production. Landlords in class-based societies were the ruling class because they controlled entrée to the land while they did not contribute to production. Meanwhile, they required the peasant producers to agree to pay part of what was produced as rent as a condition of their access to land.

The demands of the landlords were backed by the state and its tax system which came into existence coincidently with class rule. The state reflected the concentrated power of the ruling class helping to organise and maintain its power. The peasant producers resisted landlord and state demands for surplus as best they could. Faced with the constant demand for more rent the goal of peasant producers was not to increase production but to preserve and reproduce the peasant household. This conflict over the amount and disposition of the surplus was the basis of the class struggle in pre-capitalist societies and was the source of such economic dynamism that the tributary mode had. Upper class demands for rent and state taxation could increase output within limits. Over-exploitation which was common could bring ruin to the producers but also the elites.

The tributary mode of production is largely rural though it is subordinated to and produces for and interacts with urban fortresses and market centres. In most cases urban elites including merchants, landlords and state bureaucrats tend to drain and concentrate surpluses from the countryside. A historical antagonism develops between town and country.

Wealth is primarily associated with tangible objects, most importantly land. Slavery and debt bondage are tools used to tie producers to specific rulers or owners. Patriarchy is also prevalent, demanded in some measure by the necessity of passing on private property in a closely structured manner, inheritance being the operative principle. This is essential if social relations are to be reproduced across generations. If, as Althusser maintains, for capitalism ideology is a key to social reproduction, it may be that private property is among the first forms of ideology to come with societies based on social hierarchy, that being the tributary mode of production. Technology is oriented to agricultural production and distribution; innovations pass relatively slowly to other regions.

Culture is dominated by institutional spiritual organisations called religions, and this mode of production gives rise to all the major religious systems that still function: Buddhism, Judaism, Christianity, Islam, Hinduism. Belief systems are necessarily linked to institutions, social praxis and economic life in more or less complex ways.[4] Cyclical repetition and renewal tend to be a more important intellectual grounding principle than progress or accumulation. Societies tend to be sustainable over millennial scales, though particular dynastic entities rarely last more than a few centuries. Although spectacle logic is deployed, especially by the ruling institutions of church and state, forms of culture that emphasise communal relations or that ideologically and temporarily overturn hierarchy (as in the famous charivari) also operate, as does a subculture antagonistic to official religious doctrines. Socially, people are community-oriented though a wide range of individual skills and a degree of self-sufficiency is not uncommon. The ability to make ethical distinctions and have discerning judgement are demanded by the face to face social context in which an individual's reputation can be a critical feature conditioning their membership in a community. Individuals are frequently deeply connected to particular locations and home is a central value and concept, as is family lineage. Time and space are organised along the rhythm of agricultural seasons and logistics, with both hav-

4 Haldon 2015, p. 205.

ing therefore an organic quality. Pastoralists can be seen as a nomadic and entirely rural form of the tributary mode of production, often associated with grassland ecologies.

In the case of early modern India, China, the absolutist states of Europe, the Ottoman Middle East and colonial Latin America, for example, a strong central government was the main means of extracting surplus. Local landlords as well as towns, merchants and estates were subordinated to them. On the other end of the spectrum, as for example in early mediaeval feudalism, local landlords and their networks controlled most of the surplus and the central authority was weak. Under such circumstances violence was ubiquitous, harming and cowering the primary producers. On the other hand, in the Late Middle Ages the situation reversed itself. When the central authority weakened, the peasantry went on the offensive against the landlords, forcing them to shelter themselves by the authority of the centralised territorial state.

3 Asiatic Mode of Production

As we noted in broad terms, the two situations of a highly centralised state and a decentralised state correspond to the Marxian concepts of the 'Asiatic mode of production' and the 'feudal mode of production'. These concepts have been seen as enduring modes of production characteristic of Asian and Western European society. We have emphasised, following Amin and Wolf, that they should be seen as two versions of a single mode of production, the tributary mode. Hence, what Marx said about what he called the Asiatic mode of production is in our view a still useful discussion of one of the forms of the tributary mode.

It was Marx himself who first discussed the Asiatic mode. Marx's conception of Asian societies was coloured by a Eurocentric view of politics and history. Lacking grounding in the specific historical characteristics of non-European societies, he used the conception of the Asiatic mode to explain the failure of China and India to follow the capitalist road. Marx's negative view of Asia was founded on a universalist view of inevitable human progress based on the model of Western capitalism. His adverse view of Asian history was conditioned initially by the influence of Hegel's Eurocentric conception of world history and contemporary politics. Hence, although it has drawn and deserved criticism as a Eurocentric conceptual structure, it still deserves our attention.

Unlike other modes which had their own laws of motion Marx's sense of the Asiatic mode was of its immobility or absence of real historical change. In his view, this was the result of the imposition of a despotic state on top of tribal societies in which there was no private property. The ruler who in theory possessed all land extracted surplus in the form of tribute. Surplus was appropriated through officials of the subordinate state apparatus from self-sufficient largely agricultural communities. These officials had no independent economic base.

Over time, Marx came to put more stress on these rural communities than on their rulers. In these self-sufficient communities there was no private property in land, complex division of labour or much external trade. Economic surplus was limited. Trade did not disrupt the natural unity of agriculture and handicrafts. Within the village, artisans exchanged their manufactured products for food supplied by peasants. Communal property in land dated back to the earlier phase of tribal property holding. Control of village property was theoretically vested in the ruler. The tribute levied on the villages was a token of this claim. The necessity for irrigation and the state's role in providing hydraulic works also played a part in Marx's thinking about the existence of the Asiatic mode. While class society did not exist the state was able to pump surpluses out of the rural communities. As a result, he thought that the surpluses produced were greater than in what he called tribal society.

For Marx, the existence of classes based on control of property was key to the progressive evolution of history. Class struggle, the demands of the upper classes for more surplus and the resistance of the lower classes, was the motor of historical development. The overall absence of classes based on private property in the Asiatic mode was what explained its (presumed) lack of dynamism. The power of the state impeded the emergence of private property. State officials were not able to translate their high status and greater access to consumption to rights of landlordship. Instead, the despot served to guarantee the maintenance of the agrarian village communities. Political upheaval was common to these societies but underneath they were characterised by social and economic immobility. The intrusion of the West – however brutal – was necessary to end the stagnation of these societies according to Marx.

In the 1960s, the Asiatic mode experienced a revival at the hands of anthropologists who were close to the French Communist Party. These French scholars insisted that the Asiatic mode of production should not be seen as confined to Asia. Rather it should be understood as pertaining to nearly all societies in which class was emerging but had not yet crystallised. As such the Asiatic mode has wide application to the analysis of many societies, including those of Asia, the Middle East, Africa and pre-Columbian America. The Asiatic mode of production was accordingly seen by this French anthropological school as useful in describing the evolution from non-class tribal society (what we call the bush mode of production) to early class societies. In this view, the subordinate state apparatus eventually crystallised into a ruling class. The concept Asiatic mode of production would certainly seem to be useful in analysing ancient society as well as India, not to speak of Maya, Aztec and Inca societies. On the other hand, it should be understood as a conception which is subordinate to the notion of an overall tributary mode. The fusion of the latter with the concept of the Asian mode represents a major advance in widening understanding of the global history of humanity.

It should be said that our greater knowledge (in the West, developed over the last century), of the complexities and historical flux in, for example, ancient China seem to indicate that, as early as the Han empire, class played a significant role in social change (the Han, when they assumed power, entered the palace in the garb of ordinary people; their leader came from a remote village). The rise and fall of the imperial dynasties after the Warring States Period (Qin to Han to Six Dynasties to Sui to Tang to Five Dynasties to Song to Yuan to Ming and Qing) certainly involved periods of great dynamism and even incipient capitalism at points. Through all this, the contestation with northern nomadic 'military machines' drove a certain amount of interest in military innovation; and when the northerners 'won', as with the Mongols, they made their own inflections on social and political life. The influx of Buddhism to a social field previously dominated by Confucian thought, along with the emergence of Daoism, created a complex set of institutional religions vying for dominance. Since previous religions owned the best temple land, Buddhists started with temples in remote mountain areas: it may be apocryphal but some would have it that water mills were first invented out of that context. In the southeast, from the Tang period, merchant capital and even precapitalist factory production created an extensive market relation throughout the South Pacific. The railings of Chinese classical historians (such as Sima Qian, but one finds it in much of the great works) against wealthy merchants is itself a sign of their presence and power: Qian lived in the time of the Han, so he partly discredited the previous, founding Qin emperor by suggesting he was actually the progeny of a businessman who gave his secretly early-pregnant concubine to the Qin prince who later rose to the heights of power. These are just a few partial examples to suggest that ancient China was as dynamic a tributary form as could be found, riven in fact with class conflict and periods of both dynamic change and stagnation, as was the case with Europe for much of the period when it was dominated by forms of the tributary mode of production.

4 The Other Transition

In recent decades, there has been an attempt to theorise the transition not from feudalism to capitalism but the transition from antiquity to Western European feudalism, in which the notion of the tributary mode plays a key role. The feudal mode based on rent rather than tax was considered by Samir Amin as a distinct Western variant of the tributary mode. The consensus is that Western feudalism was introduced based on the initiatives of the old Roman and new Germanic landlord class. Perry Anderson initiated the discussion of the transition from Roman imperial rule to West European feudalism. In his view, there was a long period between the fall of the Western Empire and the crystallisation of feudalism. Over the centuries, feudalism developed out of a slow fusion of Germanic and Roman social and legal elements. As part of this process, the extensive use of slavery in the tributary mode of production was replaced by serfdom.

A radically different view was put forward by Guy Bois who argued that the use of slavery in the tributary mode remained dominant until the tenth century. Feudalism including the dominance of serf labour developed out of a movement in the tenth century of a religious fraction of the landlord elite known as the Cluniac monks. Upset by the secular overlord's control of the Church and the resultant corruption of religion, the Cluniacs, among other measures, took the peasants under their protection and gained their support. The secular overlords resisted and the resultant anarchy led to the consolidation of feudalism.

5 The Mediaeval Period

The English mediaevalist Chris Wickham, by contrast, sees feudalism as already existing at the beginning of the fourth century and dominant by 700 A.D. Reflecting a common view, Wickham believed that in order to avoid onerous Roman taxation peasants placed themselves under the protection of lords in the late Empire. Janus Banaji, to the contrary, insists on the continuity between Roman slaves and the manorial labour force of the emerging Dark Ages. The latter were not, as Wickham thinks, already mediaeval serfs with some control over production but rather more like slaves given a minimum of land to maintain themselves while required to do estate labour. Legal norms based in Roman law played a large role in determining their status. Hence the distinction between the slave and tributary mode is not simply an economic matter.

Wickham initially saw feudalism as distinct from the tributary mode which, for example, dominated the Eastern Roman Empire. But eventually he accepted the idea that it was a variant of the tributary mode, confirming Amin's perspective. Wickham's view represents a fundamental break from a Eurocentric historiographic conception of feudalism dating from the eighteenth century. Indeed, harking back from feudalism to Classical Antiquity, Wickham amalgamated the slave, feudal and tributary forms. All were based on the landlord or master receiving surplus from either slaves, serfs or dependent peasants. To be sure, such exploitation was carried out under different political forms, empires, kingdoms, and city-states. Ruling class ideologies were largely religious or metaphysical. In all cases the dynamic of the tributary system was the maintenance and enhancement of upper-class consumption. The development of the forces of production and generation of increasing amounts of surplus was driven by the demands made on the producers by the consumption demands of landlords and by state taxation. Feudalism was less oppressive on the peasantry than the Roman state. Most work, including that on large estates, was done by dependent peasants. Slavery and wage work existed but they were not important.

Wickham, echoing Amin, also argues that a mode of production relying on peasants existed over parts of Northern Europe, Spain and North Africa during the early Middle Ages. Marshall Sahlins refers to such societies as characterised by a domestic mode of production. In the absence of an established ruling class and state, it based itself on tribal communities, economic production below potential, reciprocal exchange between households and a stress on leisure and consumption. It represents a throwback to pre-state Neolithic communities. In the Early Middle Ages, the state scarcely existed in tribal kingdoms like England, Ireland and Denmark. It was relatively weak in Gaul, Italy and Spain. It was in these regions that the peasant mode was strongest. The weakening of the centralised state allowed the peasants to keep more of the surplus.

A commentary on Wickham by Carlos Astaria suggests that the peasant version of the tributary mode prevailed from 400–800 A.D. with the aristocracy forced to negotiate terms with various peasantries. The logic of feudalism began to take over between 800–1000 and only became fully dominant in 1000–1300. There was an ongoing development of forces of production under feudalism. The level of economic output surpassed that of the Ancient World. Increasing surpluses in agriculture and artisanal manufacture were due largely to ongoing pressure of lords for higher rents to enhance lifestyle.

6 Late Mediaeval Crisis

There was a crisis of feudalism in Western Europe 1300–1450 due to over-exploitation and the widespread revolt of peasantries and towns. Bois's interpretation is directly inspired by an Althusserian structuralism which sees it as part of a cycle of crises and recoveries based on the structure of the feudal version of the tributary mode. Bois's treatment is distinctive for emphasising the importance of peasant resistance as against landlord demands. The peasantry during the High Middle Ages undermined rent or the feudal levy by organising themselves at the village level against demands for more labour. Landlords at first reacted by inventing new forms of rent or forcing technological improvements (windmills, watermills, etc.) and later by pillage and warfare, and by eventually looking to the state for succor. In the end, the development of the early modern state (1500–1789) allowed landlords to recover and to begin a new cycle of exploitation and resistance. Bois's analysis suggests the continuity of class struggle from below throughout pre-modern French history.

7 Early Modern Feudalism

In conformity with the notion of the co-existence of different modes within a given social formation capitalism (as well as plantation slavery) developed as a subordinated mode within feudalism or the tributary mode after 1500 and allowed the latter to enjoy a second life. Indeed, in the very period which marked the ascent of capitalism between the sixteenth and nineteenth century, feudalism reconsolidated itself west of the Elbe River in Germany and extended eastward as far as Russia. While in the West serfdom continued to decline, it began to make inroads on lordships in Eastern Europe for the first time.

Between 1550 and 1720, most of Europe was feudalised or re-feudalised. This period was marked by wars and economic and demographic regression which were more pronounced in Central and Eastern Europe than in the West. Especially after 1620, and for the next one hundred years, the overall economic and demographic conjuncture was negative. Faced with these troubles, the landlord class responded with social and political reaction, especially through the growing power of the state. The frequent wars between the European powers encouraged what has been called the military revolution in the form of more sophisticated weapons and fortifications, as well as larger armies and navies. Gunpowder and cannon also enhanced the power of the Mughal Empire and the Qing rulers of China. The rural population paid the price in the form of the devastation of the countryside and heavy taxation. The regression of Eastern Europe toward serfdom and semi-colonial status was affected by the increasingly unequal exchanges between the capitalist periphery and core.

8 Slavery

Slavery already existed under the Asiatic model of the tributary mode and is today seen as part of the tributary and also even the capitalist mode. Indeed, Marx and Engels traced it back to tribal societies, suggesting that the slave could be found as part of the original family household made up of dependents including wives and children. On the other hand, however true that may be, it is important to understand the slave as someone excluded from the kinship group, the stranger with no rights in the community, whether based on kinship, citizenry or race. This view is strongly propounded by Orlando Patterson who has defined slavery as 'social death' and reviews slave practices across a vast range of time and space, although he does not pay particular attention to how dynamics might be different across distinct modes of production.

Marx, who had a thorough classical education and who therefore inherited the special interest of educated Europeans in the Greeks and Romans, treated slavery in Ancient Greece and Rome as a distinct mode of production. According to him, direct forced labour was the foundation of the Ancient World. In slavery, wealth confronted forced labour not in the form of capital but rather as a relation of direct domination. As long as slavery was predominant, the capital relationship could only be sporadic and subordinate, never dominant. In slavery, the slave is not a subject who can choose to sell her labour power or not, but is rather an instrument or tool available to work at the will of her master.

Marx's view of ancient slavery was elaborated in G.E.M. de Ste. Croix's *The Class Struggle in the Ancient Greek World* (1981). Ste. Croix saw ancient or chattel slavery as one form of unfree labour which included serfs and debt bondsmen. In Ancient society, the use of slave labour varied in place and time. The great ages of slavery were the fifth and fourth centuries in Greece, and in the Roman world the second and first centuries before Christ. These were centuries of war, conquest and flourishing commerce, including the trade in slaves. The late Roman Empire saw a decline in slave labour and an increase in the use of serfs.

Marx, Engels, Ste. Croix and others maintained that slavery was a mode of production in its own right. But the salience they gave to the slave mode of production came under criticism. Critics pointed out that, except for brief periods, the dominant mode of extraction in classical antiquity had been the collection of rent from a dependent peasantry rather than slavery. In response, the leading modern exponent of the slave mode, Ste. Croix, argued that the extraction of surplus from slave labour had been the way the ruling class in Greece and Rome at their zenith had been able to maintain its rule. Slavery was the means by which Greek city-state elites and Roman patricians extracted the surplus that enabled them to dominate politically and culturally. Moreover, their inability to fully exploit peasants who actively resisted them led them to seek slaves to exploit instead.

There are those of an empirical bent who question the existence of a slave mode of production altogether. Carlos Garcia Mac Graw, for one, is skeptical of the existence of such a mode in the Roman Empire. He denies that the largest portion of the income of the upper class overall came from the exploitation of slaves. Most of the workers on the large estates were not formally slaves, he insists. Moreover, the sheer variety of ways that so-called slaves were linked to the means of production (estate labour, rent, leasing out of slaves, domestic labour) rules out the idea of a single slave mode. Fundamentally, Mac Graw denies the utility of abstraction in historical research losing sight of the difference between the abstract nature of a mode of production and social formations containing more than one mode of production and different orders of determination. The latter is the site of class struggle and actual historical change. The former illuminates the underlying development of the forces and relations of production, along with the concomitant cultural tendencies required.

Ancient slavery, we conclude, was a mode contained within a larger social formation whose major form of exploitation was based on the exploitation of the peasant class. State taxation and direct exploitation of slave labour were the principle means of surplus extraction. This co-existence of slavery and the peasant-landlord or tributary mode raises the whole question of the historical co-existence of different modes of production. Slavery evidently can exist as a subordinate element in the tribal (though we would argue to a very limited degree, rarely if at all as a systemic feature) but also in the Asiatic and even the capitalist mode.[5]

Eric Williams initiated the discussion of the relationship between the rise of capitalism and slavery. We should take some space to discuss this connection, the more so in that the relationship between slavery and capitalism has today become a central historiographical issue. Williams's view was that industrial capitalism was made possible by the profits derived from plantation slavery in the New World. This view has been confirmed and developed by contemporary historians, especially by Robin Blackburn. Contrary to a view that has become common in mainstream historiography, that plantation slavery was itself a form of capitalism, Blackburn echoes Marx in seeing it as a form of

5 Da Graca and Zingarelli 2015, p. 7.

direct forced labour in the colonies. Under slavery, labour could not express itself as abstract labour for sale as a commodity to be transformed into surplus value. Based on a tie of personal servitude, it only permitted the extraction of surpluses which augmented the extraction of surplus value through economic exploitation or wage labour in Europe. Plantation slavery became the mechanism which allowed a process of extended primitive accumulation in the colonies, which itself fed capitalist accumulation based on the exploitation of wage labour in England and Western Europe. Forced or slave labour which was increasingly organised and intensified reinforced the extraction of surplus value at the centre. Citing scattered comments by Marx, repeated attempts have been made to view slavery as equally efficient as wage labour and to portray plantation slavery as effectively capitalist. But recent research reveals that value per se could not be extracted from forced labour and that the law of value did not govern the operation of the slave plantation which remained backward technologically.

The slaves themselves were, of course, treated as absolute commodities to be exchanged on the market, as opposed to proletarian workers who effectively sold/sell themselves. The enormous slave trade was also a significant contributor of the wealth that would be needed for capitalism to 'take off'. Of the three elements that Marx used to characterise the proletariat in *Capital* (free, rightless and rootless), it is striking that two apply directly to slaves. The brutal imposition of 'rootlessness' on African slaves would ultimately mean that after slavery they became perfect cannon fodder for capitalist exploitation.

Slavery was largely concentrated in the rural sector in North America, whereas there were many slaves in the colonial cities of Latin America and the Caribbean. Where it was found, urban slavery was likely to allow a little more autonomy to the slave. New world markets and raw materials vitally contributed to industrial capitalism. The planters, their brokers, and merchants were also crucial sources of credit helping to finance canals, railroads, and steam ships. Meanwhile, in Africa, massive imports of European guns fueled slave-raiding and an immense expansion of the slave trade in the later half of the eighteenth century. The African slave states were tributary states in which kin or lineage relations played a main part. Patterson has indicated that the possibility of manumission (purchasing or otherwise earning freedom) was an important feature in allowing for distinctions among slave societies, noting that plantation slaves in the American south had no such option.

Racism in the West certainly existed prior to the blossoming of plantation slavery. It was deeply reinforced by its success. The Haitian Revolution was the first breach in the slave regime. The eventual victory of the Haitian insurgents helped to re-invigorate the British abolitionist movement and to alarm slaveholders throughout the Western hemisphere. But paradoxically, with the ending of slavery in British and French Caribbean, and the closing of much of Spanish South America to slavery, we see a rise, not a fall, in slave numbers and the value of slave output. Between 1815 and 1860, the slave population of the Americas doubled and plantation output tripled. This second slavery flourished as a result of the worldwide demand for cotton, sugar, tobacco, rice and coffee. Extremely strong in the United States, second slavery came into conflict with industrial capitalism, abolitionism and the free labour ideology and was eventually extinguished. Slavery came to an end in Cuba and Brazil in the 1880s.

9 The State and the Tributary Mode

John Haldon has most developed the theoretical premises of the tributary mode emphasising the key role of the state to its function. The tributary form has existed in many parts of the world at different times in history and has predominated in historically important states like China, Japan, Russia, France and England. The state in this mode has to be seen as enjoying a certain autonomy while being constrained by the economic relationships which underlie it. States in this mode have an autonomy of practice in so far as they represent a nexus of historically specific specialised rules and ideological, cultural and religious practices. The chief characteristic of the tributary mode is the extraction of surplus in the form of rent, taxes or tribute by means of non-economic coercion (that is, force or the threat of force). Such surplus can be extracted from cities by imperial centres, from the lower landowners by 'great nobles' and from the higher nobility by their kings, from parishioners by their churches, but in the end all the surpluses come from the field work of peasants by all of the above. The extraction of surpluses in these forms reflects the degree of centralisation achieved in a given state with taxation representing the most developed form of surplus extraction characteristic of a strong centralised state.

The transformation of kin and lineage-based modes of surplus appropriation into those based on class exploitation lessens kinship ties and their associated forms of social practice. The extent of this loosening depends on historically local factors. The coincident extension of networks of coercive political and economic power across a wider social and geographic space leads to the development of state-like structures. On the other hand, this by no means suggests that localised or regional bonds of kinship and lineage do not continue to play a key role in production and distribution. The appearance of class antagonisms marks a new stage in the development of the relations of production. As objective antagonisms between social groups with regard to their relations of production evolve and crystallise, the state becomes the legislative and executive arm of the ruling class within the state. The community with its kinship and lineage structures organised as a set of clans or families with equal or equivalent rights no longer controls the means of production of exploitation and distribution. Instead, one group now exerts control over both the amount of surplus demanded and the mode of surplus appropriation. Invoking the control mechanisms of non-economic coercion, i.e., law, customary practice, religion, military force, a class now exploits the labour of other groups. Class struggle exists in all class societies. But it is the particular nature of the relationships of expropriation of surpluses and the contradictions which these involved which give tributary societies their particular form and trajectory. The underlying dynamic element which regulated tributary relations of production is the struggle for surplus between producing and exploiting classes. On the other hand, the fusion of the economic with the religious and political tended to mask class conflict.

The Byzantine state was an instance of the tributary form that endured throughout the Middle Ages. The state exacted surpluses in both cash and kind as well as through labour services. Undergirding its strength at first was a dense network of cities, continued existence of a middling class of landowners and a great number of more or less autonomous peasant communities directly subject fiscally to the state. The landowning elite never came to dominate either the central imperialist establishment or bureaucracies, as did the great landlords and military elites in the West. Indeed, it survived the invasions of the Arabs and Slavs in the seventh and eight centuries by a renewed centralisation of the state, which strengthened its control over a dependent aristocracy, village communities and organised religion. In contrast, the Muslim Umayyad Caliphate of the seventh century could not sustain itself faced by conflicts of interests between the centre and tribal and military conflicts compounded by ideological rivalries. Another Islamic state, the Ottoman Sultanate, was much more long-lived. It was able to impose tight centralised control and was able to do so by limiting the de facto property rights of landowners by clinging to the despotic conceptions of property characteristic of the Asiatic form of the tributary mode of production.

Religious or metaphysical ideology in the form of Zoroastrianisim, Islam, Buddhism, Confucianism, Judaism and Catholicism presided over and mediated by a class of educated specialists served the tributary state or even dominated it to their own ends. The mediaeval Roman Catholic Church led by the Papacy was an example of the latter. Religious ideas – imaginary representations of the actual circumstances of social existence – had the important function of justifying the hierarchical and class basis of society in both the form and content of their doctrines. Likewise, such ideas rationalised the patriarchal organisation of society and the family and the subordination of women. But in addition to religion justifying social inequality, the ruling class used notions of blood descent, tribe, caste and a naturalised sense of the tripartite ordering of society to rationalise its rule. Finally, since religious doctrine was the meaningful language of the peasantry, rebellion and even revolution were articulated as being 'true' to the doctrine against a corrupted religious hierarchy (as in the fertile ideological ferment during the English Civil War, or in a like manner to the way the rebel 'outlaws of the marsh' attempted to maintain their fealty to the emperor in China).

10 The Tributary Mode: Critique

Amin, Wolf and Haldon have been the major proponents of the concept of a tributary mode of production. But an interesting challenge to their view has been offered by Josh Holroyd who views it as a retreat from historical materialism in the face of post-colonial thought. Somewhat captiously, he begins his discussion by asserting that a faddish rejection of Eurocentrism has led to a departure from Marxism by Amin, Wolf and Haldon. But the issue is rather whether or not the concept of the tributary mode represents a real intellectual advance in thinking about the past and even the present. We think that the articulation of the tributary mode with the Asiatic and the whole history of European and non-European empires, and with the history of capitalism, demonstrates its intellectual force.

More intelligently, Holroyd objects that the concept of the tributary mode covers so much ground over so much time that it fails to capture the particularities of land holding, class relations and political structures in time and place. In some cases, as in Western feudalism, exploitation in the tributary mode leads to the dissolution of the cohesion of village communities, whereas in others, like the Asiatic mode, the opposite is true. The specificities of exploitation matter. Along these same lines, Jairus Banaji not only criticised the reduction of the complexity of social relations to class in considering a mode of production but also the use of what he described as the 'imagery' of modes of production with respect to the fall of the Roman Empire. Referring to the fact that, in describing this event, Wickham at the same time claimed that the ancient and mediaeval world belonged to the same mode of production led Banaji to complain that such a view deprives the collapse of the Empire of any historical significance. The tributary mode is in danger of becoming a static conception. We need to remind ourselves again and again that it is ultimately at the level of the social formation that actual historical change realises itself. The idea of the tributary mode of production allows for a wide variation even within the two main streams (centralised and decentralised) and the critical or defining features of the tributary mode of production remain in place for each of the varients. In this instance, the concept 'mode of production' works to focus attention – underlying all the imagined representations of heavenly mandates, warfare between competing states, distinct ecological circumstances, and many other reasons for distinct developments to take place – on the key drivers behind broader stasis or change in specific historical periods and places.

With this in mind, the tributary mode must be seen as having a historical dynamic ranging from the Bronze Age to the French Revolution. It gave rise to class struggles which in the Ancient World were more often than not won by the upper classes and ultimately led to its political extinction as a result of over-exploitation. Too often, we lose sight of the fact that the ultimate reason for the demise of the Roman Empire is that the ruling class over-exploited the slaves and peasants, leading to plague and demographic collapse. The cause of the so-called other transition is to be found here. Such a reminder is useful in the time of neoliberalism and COVID-19. In contrast the class struggles of the late mediaeval and early modern period, likewise induced by over-exploitation, led to the transition to the capitalist mode of production. The class capacity of the lower classes greatly developed in the Middle Ages as compared to Antiquity.

The concept of the tributary mode was developed as an alternative to a Eurocentric view of history. In order to ensure it does not lead to a too static view of history, allowance must be made for the variety of forms it can encompass, the overlay of residual or emergent modes of production within specific social formations, the facts of specific historical development in distinct contexts and, of particular importance in our own era, the factors behind the transition from feudalism to capitalism. The fact that capitalism was born in the West and continues to be centred there remains relevant to understanding the history of the concept of modes of production. But the concept itself has moved far beyond its original boundaries, allowing for insight into the sweep of history and into what forms of change are consequential and which amount to a reshuffling among the leadership factions of a particular social order. The idea of a tributary mode of production is a powerful tool for understanding the fundamental exploitations that grounded perhaps ten millenia of human activity, in the Global West and South alike, and provided a critical understanding of the foundation from which capitalism could eventually spring.

11 Source Note

In reaction to Eurocentrism, Amin and Wolf developed the idea of the tributary mode. The Byzantinist Haldon then elaborated its basic features. It was important that the distinguished Oxford mediaevalist Chris Wickham then abandoned the term 'feudal mode' of production in favour of the term 'tributary mode'. As it came to be understood, the tributary mode included the feudal, slave and Asiatic modes. However, the relation of the slave mode to feudalism and capitalism remains highly discussable. Moreover, Godelier has shown that the Asiatic mode is a concept that can help to shed light on societies in which classes have not differentiated themselves. Holroyd, Banaji and others meanwhile have complained that the concept of the tributary mode is too static and fails to take account of significant historical changes across millenia.

CHAPTER 4

The Bush Mode of Production

1 Introduction

The bush mode of production was described by Marx and Engels as 'primitive communism'. Bush people have been known as nomadic foragers, or gatherers and hunters, and have also been associated with the Palaeolithic era of human history (about 2.5 million years ago to about 10,000 B.C.E.). While subjected to the most deep-seated and pernicious ideological disparagement since the neolithic break (the emergence of agricultural-based tributary societies), there has been a modernist strain of sympathy towards them (Rousseau), often disparaged as 'romantic', a Marxist inflected appreciation for aspects of their social relations (both Marx and Engels, separately and together), and in recent years a mass of anthropological research findings and theorising that allow for, over the last six decades, a considerable reappraisal in line with Rousseau, Marx and Engels's speculative and politicised sympathy. The latter reappraisal is associated with the work of Eleanor Leacock, Richard Lee, Marshall Sahlins, filtering down to anthropologists working with particular bush peoples around the world and emerging from the scholarship now coming from among their ranks.

What follows will largely be a structural description rather than a historical one, though a few comments about the form of history of bush people will follow. The structural description could also be characterised as evocative – an evocation or opening onto the understanding of a distinct way of life, and as political, a deliberate deployment of a political arsenal or sensibility. We will begin with a brief review of the ideological disparagement and the issues that surround it, and then turn to several features of the bush mode of production: social relations with an emphasis on gender relations, ownership of the means of production, nomadism and its implications on property relations, the overall characterisation (by Sahlins) of bush people as 'affluent', elements of expressive culture and spirituality. The chapter will end with brief discussions of four other points: the political value of the understanding we advocate to broad socialist and feminist projects and to the political projects of bush people themselves; the emergence of scholarship from among bush peoples and the issues of representation that develop as a result; the question of history in relation to culture; and issues pertaining to bush people in the contemporary period. We conclude with a firm rejection of evolutionary social theory and a discussion of some of the ways in which bush people represent the most 'advanced' expressions of species being. We do not assign bush people to memory, some distant time in the past but rather write in the knowledge that the bush mode of production remains an aspect of contemporary global life: bush people are not a 'were', they rather are an 'are' in our account.

2 The Civilised/Savage Dichotomy

It can be said on one level that appreciation for bush people is to some extent a necessary reaction to an age-old disparagement of the bush way of life, structured into all the languages and values of tributary societies and inherited and given its own inflection under capitalism: this disparagement is called the 'Neolithic bias'. The Neolithic bias perhaps emerges from the need of farming peoples to always expand their territories by cutting into the forests of bush people, as much as their irritation at bush people's occasional tramping of their fields and insouciance regarding issues of work and survival. Whatever the source, age old prejudices against nomadism (the homeless wanderer) come to rest in the very language of 'civilisation', a term invented to raise the status of farming peoples against their neighbours, who become disparaged as 'barbarians' if they are herders and 'savage' if they are bush people. One apotheosis of this thinking is found in the early modern period, expressed by Thomas Hobbes. But it can be found, implicitly or explicitly, in all the official belief systems of the great tributary social forms: the bush people are savage, less than human, in the way of the land clearances necessary for the growth of civilisation, untrustworthy, without gods, laws or kings, miserable, violent, brutal, eaters of their own children, jealous of the comforts of civilisation, child-like, base, sexually perverse, cruel – all that is worst of the human condition is poured into the vessel of the savage, though they may also be grudgingly and paradoxically acknowledged or attributed with near-superhuman strength, endurance, stoicism, masculine brutality, even sentimentality.

It is impossible to simply set aside, displace (deconstruct), or move gently away from the force of this ancient ideology, the Neolithic bias. It must be shattered. To shatter it, it must be overturned. A clear-eyed view, that appreciates strengths and weaknesses among bush people, can only be arrived at upon such a foundation. Hence, we build upon a strain of counter-thought that questions the project of civilisation in the West, from Tacitus to Rousseau, which finds in the bush a more positive avatar of human potential. We produce a description of the bush mode that leans towards appreciation as a necessary step in the appreciation-criticism dialectic that grounds critique. Appreciation is always the first step in understanding, and is more than ever required in a context where disparagement has such ancient roots in thought and in the very structure of language.

Hobbes's infamous description sits in his social contract theory at the site of the 'state of nature', a notion or abstraction that in his view may never have actually existed in human history or 'reality'. But it rests comfortably with the notion that bush people are more 'natural', which is famously taken both as the source of their weakness or basis of their strength. In crude terms, hippies loved Indians because they lived 'closer to nature'. Our attempt is to describe bush people, although in favourable terms, without using that metaphor. The nature/culture distinction has once again reared its head in social theory[1] after some decades premised on the critical assumption that 'nature is dead'. We simply note that the metaphor of proximity to nature is useless. As the writer Italo Calvino noticed, no one is closer to nature than you, at this very moment: With your fingernails and hair growing, your eyes beginning to droop with sleep, your urge to unburden your body of its self-produced waste and your certain knowledge that you too, like all the others around you, like all who came before and will come after, of every race, class, gender, sexual preference, ability, temperament ... will die. It is preferable not to think about it. Bush people have their own language for conceiving 'nature', their ecological circumstances, their selves, as do tributary peasants and capitalist workers. It is no more present or absent in their lives, and certainly no 'closer' to them, than nature is here, now, among us as we write and you as you read. The bush mode of production is a social form and a human invention as much as late capitalism: It deploys and is limited by the inside and outside facts of what it constructs as 'nature' as much as late capitalism.

3 Features of the Bush Mode of Production I: Egalitarianism

Perhaps the most remarkable feature of bush people is the relative absence of social hierarchy or the presence of a rough equality. This feature is itself grounded in the emphatically collective project of bush sociality, and in the ethic of respect for personal autonomy that circulates so strongly. Two egalitarianisms deserve foregrounding here: that of 'public' decision making and that of gender relations normally consigned to the 'private' sphere, though that very distinction is one that breaks down under the weight of close description. Egal-

1 Moore 2015.

itarianism is here positioned as a specifically political fact, but it also colours economic relations, as we shall show when we turn to collective ownership of the means of production.

Anthropologists have strongly tended to agree that leadership among hunting bands is weak, by which they mean there are no 'bosses' in everyday life, little inheritance of political privilege. Pierre Clastres points out the general, quotidian rule that 'no one can give an order with an assurance that it will be followed'. Leadership, such as it is, is situational: A good seamstress will offer guidance in a large-scale community sewing project, an acknowledged caribou hunter will draw up the plan of approach in a specific hunting situation. Often the person with the most experience assumes such a role, and often that is the oldest person, the elder. Even in these circumstances, another seamstress might interject with a suggestion, which then gets discussed. The caribou hunter may be less successful as a sea mammal hunter and defer to another's authority or ability in such a circumstance. No doubt among hunters, as among peasants and workers, everyone has different strengths and weaknesses. Some may be happier to be guided, and others delight in the burden of decision making. But key decisions are made collectively: Everyone, or at least the overwhelming majority, must be satisfied with the decision for it to take effect. An idea, a solution, a compromise, can come from any quarter. Politics in such a situation is much more complex than it is in hierarchical societies; hierarchy allows for simplicity, chains of command, everyone's place predetermined: It encourages thought to come to a halt in favour of obedience. Collective egalitarianism demands situational adaptability and reflection on the part of every single member of the specific collective. Therefore, it requires every member of the collective to cultivate discernment, judgement, independent thought.

The general rule – that no one can give a command with any assurance that it will be followed – extends to or from gender relations. Women and men in heterosexual couplings generally do not control each other's work. While there is a sexual division of labour – women as gatherers, men as hunters most commonly – each side has control over its sphere. The men do not presume to tell the women how to do their jobs, the women do not presume to tell the men. The sphere of women's work includes child care, food preparation, care of the hearth, gathering of plant-based food, clothing preparation, sometimes hunting of small animals and birds, often fishing. Globally, when bush people lived in the temperate and lushest parts of the world, most bush people's diet was plant based, so women's food production work was of equal or larger importance than men's work. Meat was often prized simply because it involved a rarer portion of the diet. Some activities had a very different inflection in the social context of bush life. For example, child rearing in late capitalism is an onerous a job as can be found, particularly because it is so often so isolating. When you have a child today, you should have a formal ceremony saying 'goodbye' to all your friends because you really won't be seeing them anymore. Among bush women, when you have a child you gain respect and join the circle of mothers. All the mothers and the older children (male or female) are attentive to any of the young children that wander into their sight-line, in a social landscape often structured as a circle around a common and safe work/play/ceremonial space. Strong women could and did become camp leaders: the facilitators of major decisions, respected for their knowledge and wisdom. Lineages could be traced on the mother's or father's side, and patri- or matrilocality could be practiced. Divorce was acceptable without stigma. Inheritance hardly mattered, so maintenance of virginity was not a strict requirement, women's bodies did not have to be policed. While it cannot be doubted that there were men or women who violated these norms, they were the norms: In the daily run of affairs, women co-operated with other women and controlled their sphere of work, as did men, and while each partnership had its own dynamic – a charismatic or highly respected partner of one sex might somewhat overshadow their partner more or less – these dynamics were developed in a context that can only be described as egalitarian.

In such a decentred decision-making context, political egalitarianism implied or embodies a kind of participatory democracy, a democracy without votes and without representation. This presupposes and founds a notion of respect for personal autonomy. Every person's dignity meant that the default social value was respect. Each person had to be able to make up their own mind, calculate their own positionality, own their own ground. A highly respected leader or elder would quickly lose the respect of the people around them if they began to act in an arrogant or haughty manner. Respect for personal autonomy extended among women and men and extended even to children. There is no age of majority that allows a young person's thoughts to be ignored. The wishes of children are treated seriously, though most no doubt feel it would be presumptuous to state a position on a group decision until they have begun to take on a role of responsibility. The deep-seated notion of respect for personal autonomy means that gender identifications across sexual identifications may not lead to diminution of value, and certainly some bush peoples had socially sanctioned and named identifications for such positionalities.

Where every individual is a part of a group focused on achievement or maintenance of a good life, the need to recognise the contribution of every other, to support those who have a weaker ability, to appreciate those with a greater, to have the sensitivity of sorting who is who among these, to raise each other up as part of the process of raising all to the best that can be, to nurture the children in a loving way so they in turn will nurture with love your own later and weaker years, where these are the daily fact of existence, meaningful egalitarianism can thrive. It is a complex social and political reality: Far more complex capacities are demanded of each member than in tributary and capitalist modes. Such a politics rests upon and itself founds the other economic and social facts or features of the bush mode of production.

4 Features of the Bush Mode of Production II: Communism

Yes, communism is a dirty word these days. Here we deploy it as an economic descriptor for common ownership of the means of production, though 'ownership' should be understood as an external descriptor. The land that was a base for bush people was a common property to such a degree that it can hardly be called a property at all: It was what Marx termed an inorganic appendage, a prothesis, a part of the self. Bush people 'owned' land the way we 'own' our eyes. While some more or less defined land allocations or allotment systems may have sorted out who – which family or clan – gathered or hunted in what rough locations, both within those allocations and as regards the whole 'national' territory the means of production were the responsibility of the people who produced a good life from those means. No lord or bishop ruled the whole, no corporate entity was charged with extraction of every possible commercial facet. Furthermore, the tools that one needed in order to work a territory were made by each individual engaged in that work from readily available materials. The knowledge of how to make and use the tools, and the creative inventiveness to explore better ways of doing so, were also freely available, passed on from parent to child.

The rules of sharing involved free sharing of more essential elements of life and free sharing among closer relations, with more private and less essential items less likely to be freely shared, and less close social ties also reducing the obligation to share. Food might be shared with strangers, but not an element from your sacred bundle; the latter might be passed on to a daughter or son or apprentice at an appropriate life stage. While all the forms of reciprocity circulated, generalised or gift reciprocity was the daily or normal social reality.

In this context, no individual or family was significantly materially better off than any other. A general egalitarianism also prevailed on the economic level. While very small differences *may* have had magnified social importance, allowing some to feel better off than others, or more hard-working, or more successful, for the most part these differences were materially slight and from season to season, certainly generation to generation, could be overturned. Hence it was best not to become too full of oneself or to demean those around you. The best hunters always attributed their success to luck, and emphatically refused to boast about their success. A good life could not be achieved by an individual or nuclear family, it was the condition of the village or band as a whole: difficult and easy situations were shared by all.

5 Features of the Bush Mode of Production III: Nomadism

While the image of endless, and perhaps aimless, wandering is a strong element in the systematic assault of bush people in the thought structures of tributary and capitalist modes of production, nomadism in the practice of bush people is anything but endless or aimless. Normal circumstances involved a nomadism within a flexibly but also well-defined territory and involved seasonal use of resources. A seasonal cycle (and each ecological user group determined what those seasons were) meant movement to a fishing site, onwards to berry or root or nut patches, onwards again to a hunting ground or a season of wandering over a hunting ground, and perhaps back to the fishing camp. Such oscillations might be dual or multiple, depending upon the ecology of the specific territory. As a result, it is necessary to abandon the notion of an 'aimless' and 'endless' nomadism, and specifically the notion that nomadism means homelessness. Rather, one's intimately well-known territory is the home, not a site-specific location.

For all the foregoing, nevertheless nomadism does involve regular intervals of travel, and this has extraordinary social consequences. One of these is that the tools of mobility in many contexts become vital elements of daily life, and to be able to extend mobility can imply a better life quality. The formula that territory covered can equal calories counted, at least in certain ecologies, means each group gives attentiveness to the material bases of transportation, from feet to elaborate ocean-going vessels. A good deal of time in any life cycle is based on making or repairing transportation tools as well as in the process of movement. Furthermore, seasons themselves are associated with areas within a territory: Spring is not a change simply in weather, but a change in place, as is every other season – and there may be more or less than four of these – that the specific ecological and social dynamic constructs.

To be frequently mobile involves a severe restriction on the ability to accumulate material goods or objects. With no permanent yard, shed, closet, basement, field, room in which to pile stuff, there is no need for stuff to pile. A material fact conditions a structure of property relationship. Objects become, literally, burdens. In this social context, gift giving is enormously difficult, hence a highly prized art form to such a degree that Marcel Mauss can see it as a defining feature. The valence of how the object world itself is actually seen shifts. While in both tributary and capitalist circumstances objects are viewed through a lens of desire, nowadays endlessly provoked, among bush people objects are viewed with something more like suspicion: first and foremost, as weight, a burden that one wants to have a good reason for carrying. This fact conditions or is a presupposition of the rough economic egalitarianism described above: People's ability to have wealth differences is limited to what more they can carry. Material wealth is not a valued attribute but, if anything, a source of pity.

6 Features of the Bush Mode of Production IV: Affluence

Marshall Sahlins has called the bush mode of production 'The Original Affluent Society' in an invaluable and well-known essay of the same name. While his arguments rest in part on the features discussed above, he adds two characterisations: minimal need structure and extensive leisure time. These each deserve some attention.

By minimal need structure, Sahlins argues that people can be well off, or even wealthy, if their needs are easily met. If new needs are not endlessly invented and provoked, when the spirit of social hierarchy is not driving a competitive urge, where something other than the object domain is the well spring of a good life, generalised affluence is at least possible. Among bush people, where everyone can make the tools they need with their own hands, when mobility replaces the desire for things with a suspicion of things, and if well-being of the group is a precondition of well-being of the self, generalised affluence is realised in daily life and named as such: the good life. This good life is compounded because of the abundance that prevailed in the ecologies occupied by bush people: There were plenty of nuts, berries, fish, and animals to such an extent that bush people saw no need to hoard or elaborately store or extensively worry – the land would provide. The land could be adjusted – weirs built, fire used to clear parts of the forest – in smaller or larger ways that would improve the lot of future generations. Some food storage practices such as drying meat could secure people over seasonal periods of want. Patterns could adapt with grand changes in climate or other social or ecological developments. But as long as wealth did not demand an accumulation of things, as long as contentment and happiness came from the respect and admiration of others, from the ability to be expressive creatively, from the joy of one's children or siblings or partners, from the feel of the sun or wind or water, from the sure knowledge of self-strength and health, and from, finally, the time one could give to these dimensions of life, wealth was achievable and, more often than not, very likely achieved.

That last of these features was given particular attention by Sahlins, who also discusses the 'extensive leisure time' of bush people. The argument, in brief, is that bush people spend much less time per day in productive labour than modern industrial workers (or than the even longer work-days of peasants). Sahlins compiles studies that show, on average, a three to four-hour work day for men, sometimes in extended work binges followed by even more extended relaxation binges. He does not account for women's work, especially child rearing, and to some degree even the work-leisure boundary becomes porous among bush people. What work they often did – fishing, hunting, berry picking – are leisure activities for aristocrats and businessmen alike. The actual quality of productive work, under the control of each worker's ability and temperament, is dramatically different among bush people. Sahlins notes that bush people seem to extensively enjoy the privilege of 'daytime sleep', no doubt also a precondition to good health. But we note as well that much of the extra 'leisure' time may have been turned to the extraordinarily rich creative expressions produced by bush people. Time is the most fundamental precondition of a good life. When you have enough time to give to your family, your community, yourself, when you can rest, contemplate, discuss, bask, you are enjoying what is by far most precious: Your limited span as a conscious being, a span that will come to an end. Whatever of that span you have that is not owned by your boss or lord, that you do not have to expend in your struggle to exist, this is the most meaningful form of wealth you can be said to possess. Marx knew this. As does Sahlins. Bush people were wealthy in part because, of all other social forms, they provided for the most socially generalised amounts of time under the control of each of the individuals who comprised the society.

7 Features of the Bush Mode of Production v: Expressive Culture and Spirituality

Out of this time grew, not only healthy and extended daytime nap cycles, but a remarkably rich cultural and spiritual life. While oral narrative was perhaps among the highest form of cultural expression, song, dance, decorative arts, image making, design, architecture, games, also flourished. The discussion of spiritual questions in everyday life and in ceremonial life was also a by-product of temporal wealth. It might be noted that the intellectual demands of daily life, the skills required to tan a hide or hunt an animal, when coupled with the temporal wealth, have led many contemporary hunters to succeed as individual artists. But technology itself was not distinct from art: most of the tools of bush people are now more often appreciated as art objects for the grace, balance and elegance they embody. The time of the bush mode of production was, socially, the finest time in the history of humankind for creative expression.

The feature of expressive culture and of ceremonial and spiritual life we want to emphasise are embedded in the forms of these. The spiritual or social structures and events are most often circular: a men's house, a sweat lodge, a drum dance or pow wow, a *qaggiq*. This circular structure of architecture and bodies in our view expresses the egalitarianism so pervasive within the social, political and economic dimensions of life. While individuals may have gained particular respect for their spiritual powers or knowledge, the forms in which these were expressed and shared connoted and enacted egalitarianism in the profoundest manner: a sharp difference from the hierarchies and spectacle logic that pervade institutionalised spiritualities.

The creative richness of bush peoples did not escape the notice of cultural modernity. Modern art pillaged from the wealth-spring of bush-based creativity, while at the same time sitting upon an ideological foundation that emphasised savage primitivism incapable of so-called abstract thought. But, straight from the well of temporal wealth, powerful cultural and artistic expressions were drawn: In them, the highest possibilities of human achievement can, as if one sees a reflection in the deep darkness or hears a pebble splash so far below, be gleaned.

8 The Global History of the Bush Mode of Production

Homo sapiens have been building tools for about two and half million years. Modern people, *homo sapiens sapiens*, have been around for somewhere between 160,000 and 90,000 years. Taking the later date, even the very last, 90,000 years: The bush mode of production represents by far the most sustainable way of life human beings have ever invented. The bush way of life did not disappear 12,000 years ago; many aspects of it have continued into the present, deepening relations with ecological settings, adapting and using very different kinds of technologies, responding to by resisting or accommodating colonial intrusions, which also at times succeeded in genocidal eradications or assimilations. The struggles of bush people in the contemporary historical moment deserve a special attention for the social base they can provide as intergenerational communities of production and as embodied holders of values that will need to be shared more widely.

Here is the story we are telling: For millenia, bush people thrived across the world. Social or natural events led them to new ecological homes, to geographic dispersion. New tools, new stories, were invented. Distinct bush people traded, and no doubt at times fought bitter battles. Distinct peoples slowly changed, adapting to newer settings or changes in older ones, and adapting to each other. Strong personalities, charismatic leaders and even lineages, rose and fell, over untold generations. Large villages developed in response to collective needs – whale hunting, for example – and dispersed with seasons or time. Bush people thrived in the most nurturing of ecological settings, tropical coasts for example, but also thrived in what appear to us as marginal ecological settings: deserts, deep jungles, subarctic and arctic lands. Very lengthy occupations of these lands lead to very deep understandings of them, of the varied food sources, the medicines, the materials for tools, the habits of animals, the patterns of wind and weather. Origin stories were told; the world retained its enchantment, so a strong sense of spiritual and magical efficacy developed immediately alongside a kind of determined empiricism in observation. There were conflicts, bad times, traumas. But for a long time, many and even most people under these circumstances lived a good life. We are all descended from the people of this time.

Over a few thousand years, perhaps two or three, and after many tens of thousands of years, about twelve thousand years ago, some bush people began to try taming animals and, scratching at the soil, domesticating and growing edible plants. Sometimes, after many generations, they gave up and went back to their former way of life. Sometimes, after many generations, they discovered that in order to succeed at the new game, they would need to mark off their lands and pass it on to their descendants. Some were luckier or more successful than others, able to marshal large families and supporters to husband the resources of large fields. Slowly, not inevitably, and over a very long period, a new way of life developed. This process is called the Neolithic break. For some people it offered a greater control over food security. But it also involved new values, new systems of social organisation. Property and social hierarchy developed. A new mode of production was borne from the bush mode of production: cultivation of land and husbandry of animals eventually lead to population growth, the sharpening of private property, the ossification of social hierarchy, the creation of state forms to defend the new system: the tributary mode of production.

Graeber and Wengrow, in *The Dawn of Everything*, sharply disagree with the above narrative. They give two reasons: 1. There is a good deal of evidence that early cities, some based on agriculture, some not, were egalitarian (that is, hierarchy is not directly linked to urbanisation or agriculture); 2. How can a 'revolution' or 'break' characterise a period that likely covered three thousand or more years? As regards the second of these, we have two responses: for a social form that lasted two hundred thousand years, three thousand does represent a short duration, in fact about one and a half percent of the time spent by all humans as bush people. If tributary societies are about 6000 years old, the few hundred years (an overestimate) of time that led to the transition to capitalism amounts to perhaps five percent of that period, roughly the same order of magnitude. The critical feature in assessing whether a break is revolutionary for us is the question of whether the ownership of the means of production and the new productive forces have been fundamentally altered. What Graeber and Wengrow consistently fail to mention is that fact that, after the Neolithic break, tributary societies expressive of sharp social hierarchy became the norm and agricultural egalitarianism the disappearing exception. This also represents our response to their first point: During the transitional Neolithic break many forms were tried, including urban spaces and/or agricultural communities that reflected egalitarian ideals. That one basic form, the tributary mode of production, developed with similar basic features in the Americas, in Africa, in Asia and in Europe, reminds us that structure does constrain and condition agency and that, for all their breathless bluster about entirely free social agents, the new forces of production represented by domestication and agriculture strongly implied and tended towards a social result, a change in relations of production that came to involve hierarchy, gender subordination, private property and state forms of governance.

The two modes mostly likely existed in a daily balance. Goods could be traded; the farmers made new tools, new foods, had new stories to tell. But the farmers also needed to have more land to support their larger families. They spread as a people, pushing bush people off of the most desirable arable lands. They also invented all kinds of stories to justify the cruelties involved. Bush people retained a prominent place globally, but in areas less accessible or desirable to their farming neighbours. Meanwhile, those bush people who remained did not simply stagnate: They continued to invent, to develop their capacities and understandings, to elaborate their social knowledge, their ethical practices and their ecological knowledge. While self-described civilisations rose and fell across the world, the bush people patiently went about their ways, consistently refusing to take the bait of social hierarchy. Many, indeed the vast majority of us, are descendants of the tributary societies that ascended and declined over the last six to ten thousand years.

Out of the pores of some of those tributary societies, doubling down on social hierarchy, on abstraction, something new emerged. In the lands of China, where the forests gave way to agriculture, monks were forced into the mountains for their meditations. There, they discovered the power of water. The new technologies developed within tributary societies merged with an expanded and expanding merchant presence. People were displaced from their land. Fierce civil wars over who should get what – a problem endemic to the farmers – pushed the limits on a way of life, and within a ridiculously short period, a tendency within the tributary mode of production gave way to an entirely new mode: capitalism. The bush people really did not see it coming. Their patience did not pay off. The capitalist dynamic led to interests in lands and resources and knowledges and bodies of bush people, and of farming people. The new mode of production was far more ruthless, far more totalising. It did not care about the difference between hunters and farmers: Both became colonised, Indigenous, Aboriginal, others – to be enslaved, pauperised, murdered, stripped of lands, conquered. Like their farming predecessors, the capitalists were able to develop excellent justifications for their brutal actions, to see themselves as righteous, benevolent, compassionate even. The ultimate ideological tool or justification: modernity and progress. Their reach was far vaster than that of farmers, and within a meagre few hundred years they were chasing the remaining bush people off of the very last of their land bases, to what are considered the least hospital ecologies for human habitation.

Whatever our source of descent, whether from bush people or from farmers or from capitalists, we all live under the hegemony of this newest and most totalising mode of production. After tens of thousands of years, the remaining bush people have a precarious perch on this planet. Such is the story we tell.

9 Bush History and Bush Culture: A Few Comments

Our discussion of the tributary and capitalist modes of production focussed on history, while the discussion of the bush mode of production can be characterised as more structural in orientation, mirroring the history/anthropology distinction itself. But it is not as if bush peoples have no history. The records upon which that history can be adduced include ancient oral narratives, traces of material culture long left buried in the dirt, what evidence of change over time can be gleaned from linguistics or genetics, extant images or objects that have stood for lengthy periods of time. In combination, these form an archive that tell the historical stories of the rise and fall and movement and disappearance and resurgence of distinct bush cultures or nations. Cultural continuity and change are here themselves history, so the boundary between history and culture itself also becomes porous.

So many cherished boundaries of thought can hardly be sustained the closer description comes to its referent: the bush mode of production. Work and leisure, in a context where work can be so fun, hardly can be measured against each other. The public and private, in a context where familial relations form the centre of symbolic determination and the public can be said to have wholly subsumed the private, likewise collapse. It is not unrelated that Derrida uses passages from Lévi-Strauss's *Tristes Tropiques* to challenge the distinction between speech and writing. Can culture and nature be kept distinct? Is history here not culture? In the Marxist canon, where Marx speculates that among bush people 'the community appears as the first great force of production', he thereby challenges his own invaluable distinction between forces and relations of production: Among bush peoples, the greatest force is in fact a relation.

Out of this series of challenges to foundational philosophical boundaries come a related series of paradoxes. Although bush people are clearly deeply co-operative, the respect for personal autonomy that in ethical terms grounds this communitarianism, also allows for and perhaps even encourages a striking individualism. Individual self-reliance, individual difference, idiosyncrasy, distinctiveness, all thrive in such a social context. Capitalist modernism, based on the possessive individual, everywhere heralds its individualisation and everywhere sets up structures of social docility: the cookie-cutter suburbs.

All this suggests a greater intellectual modesty is demanded in the description of particular bush people. Where cherished categorical distinctions fall mutely to the ground, where it is so easy to rush to explanation or judgement or even description, new layers of ideology accumulate upon the already noted layers of Neolithic bias. The foregoing, then, we offer as a weak and romanticised description aimed like an arrow at the heart of the Neolithic bias; our hope is that it opens onto better descriptions.

9.1 *Bush Scholars and Activists*

Such description may emerge from the work of bush scholars themselves. The academy now boasts an ability to incorporate individuals from the bush, who provide the potential of deploying new conceptual languages and new descriptive purchase. Though fewer in number than advertised – only a small minority of even Indigenous scholars actually come with a background in the bush, although another minority turns their attention to cultural description of the bush, an internal anthropology of sorts – and though the university as a structure of knowledge production and dissemination remains largely impervious to challenges from such a source and of such a profound structure, yet the social potential now does exist, increasingly, to produce description and analysis from within.

Out of such potential come concepts, like *pimatisiwin* (the good life) or *Nda-nwendaaganag* (all my relations) or the thanksgiving address or the *Inuit Qaujimajatuqangit* (Inuit knowledge) or many other intellectual treasures. At best, these may play a role in destabilising a power-knowledge nexus long comfortable on its perch as a foundation of ecological destruction and social oppression. At best, these may offer global paths through the morass of intellectual modern endgames. At best, these may once again raise the possibility of a justice that deserves the name, of the still viable opening onto the possibilities of a human project, conditioned as they are by the structures that give rise to them.

The contemporary world has also given rise to political activists who have emerged, many straight from the bush, propelled into prominence by their life and death struggle to save this or that ecological niche in its moment of being threatened by totalising processes of resource extraction in the interests of contemporary primitive accumulations. In the bodies, practices, speeches and writings of these individuals, it is possible to at times glimpse the highest of ethical aspirations our species can articulate. They do not merely exemplify; they inspire.

9.2 *The Bush Mode of Production Now*

The bush mode of production is not some feature of a quaint, outdated past. There are gathering and hunting bush people in the world today. Their lives have been changed by an unrelenting colonialism associated with the primitive accumulation requirements of modernist capitalism, with the absorption of dramatically different technological forms, through immersion in a different spiritual and value system linked to the most subtle and obvious of social elements, for example the proper name. But the twentieth century was as much a narrative of bush people's persistence as it was of bush people's often projected disappearance. Bush people became brilliant in the politically unconscious trick of social subversion. Centralisation of bush people was almost everywhere a major element of colonial capitalist state-sanctioned and enforced policy, for example. But centralisation into settlements could be undercut by use of newer technologies of mobility that allowed access to the whole traditional territory. The state 'defines' bush people as part of the practice of legalising their subservience. The bush people take this definition as a positive recognition of legal difference, and ultimately as a basis of specific rights. Using these kinds of sleight of hands, bush people pass on their values, their languages, their ways into a precarious and uncertain future. Will disappearance be the story of the twenty-first century, not just of bush people but of us all?

Some version of the description we have articulated has, for a few decades, been a part of the politics of advocacy anthropology: an honourable project too easily dismissed under the weight of intellectual fashion. We offer this in order to, again, suggest that the struggles of bush people are to be distinguished from the struggles of other rural peoples, are to be understood in terms of distinctiveness and priority in the contemporary social ecology. Bush peoples are worthy of support in their own terms as a remainder and reminder of the best of what our species being can achieve.

Somewhere at the margins of modernist capitalism, there is still bush country, by reason of its marginality or other qualities not yet subjected to the brutalities of 'natural resource' extraction. These marginal areas are a centre for each of the distinct bush peoples who occupy them. Their political struggles are vital, worthy of attention and respect, and for all the small size of their population, are struggles that raise the most profound questions that can be asked, across the deepest chasm that divides human experience: mode of production.

9.3 *Socialism and Feminism Enter the Bush*

We offer the description of the bush mode of production in the same spirit that Engels or Rousseau polemicised. They knew that an appreciation of bush people stood as a deep structural critique of the 'civilised' societies around them. Such a descriptive apparatus was a political resource. In our time, for example, Fredric Jameson has urgently, consistently and extensively written of the need for a continued discussion of utopian possibility, while resting his analytical lens on literature as its site. But anthropology is a far more invaluable site.

The capitalist mode of production has existed for about five hundred years; industrial capitalism a mere two and a half centuries. The tributary mode of production has been with humankind for perhaps twelve thousand years at most, more likely about four or five thousand: a pretty good run, compared to capitalism. The bush mode of production has been around for at least ninety thousand years and likely two hundred thousand: a whole other order of magnitude. As we noted above, if sustainability were our main standard for adjudicating the value of a social form, bush people would clearly be appreciated much, much more. Their way of life was and is the most sustainable form ever produced by the human species.

That is a simple fact, undisputed in the worlds of science, natural history, human science, though the actual dates may vary within the overall parameters suggested above. Now, if the description offered above has fidelity, we are in a position to say that social hierarchy, including gender hierarchy, is not the norm of human history but rather the exception, an anomaly that does not appear to have worked out very well. Perhaps, then, broader struggles for social justice, for gender equality, or in fact to save our life form in the context of a planet being actively reduced to an increasingly precarious stage for human life, perhaps these struggles have something to learn from the bush mode of production, some inspiration to motivate, some arguments to deploy: 'like the sound of a shell in the deep' indeed.

10 Conclusion

It is clear that we have travelled some distance from the evolutionary anthropology that still retains a remarkable hold on the social imagination. Each of the modes of production we have discussed offer resources, benefits, advantages, successes, insights, opportunities. And each has its restrictions, failures, losses, limitations, biases, challenges. It is not useful to think of the change from one to another as inevitable, progressive, always in each and every way better. Such a form of thought is part and parcel of Neolithic bias driven ever faster by capitalist modernism. And such a form of thought still has a surprising and normalising hold.

Analytically, thinking of these modes of production does provide an extraordinary purchase on the issues faced by our species. At this level of thought, the glacial level, the level of the highest horizon of interpretation (Jameson), it is possible to ask questions of and through species being. It is possible to denaturalise deeply held social assumptions – for example of inevitable male dominance or of transhistorical underlying scarcity – and to reconfigure social possibilities, at least in thought, if not in practice.

The regular riposte to this utopian view of bush people is that this mode does not work for the large urban populations of the contemporary historical conjuncture. We did not say and do not say it does, though Graeber and Wengrow do offer compelling examples of egalitarian urban spaces both in the period of the Neolithic break and in particular spaces after it (for example, Teotihuacan). Instead, to repeat, what we do say is twofold: Firstly, bush people deserve to be supported in their struggles to maintain their life ways; demographic facts, even democracy, do not trump the justice of this position. A respectable socialist who argues that the few James Bay Cree should not be allowed to interfere with the national aspirations of Quebecois workers – who we also support – is showing the same short-sightedness of every socialist project that placed the needs of bush people beneath the needs of the socialist nation. These forms of socialism look remarkably like capitalism to bush people, and have been a consistent theme of many but not all so-called socialist projects over the past century. We assert the necessity of a socialism that can find profound alliance in and with the pores of bush cultures. Secondly, bush people are a source of inspiration, a pin that punctures the balloon of docility floated on the ether of naturalised notions of hierarchy. Bush people lend ideas, weight, force to feminist and socialist thought and practice; they are an invaluable storehouse of embodied practice, performing in the smallest daily gestures a whole distinct and invaluable set of values. Last but not least, capitalist modernity surrounds us and embeds its normalising social practices as if they were 'natural': Both tributary and bush forms of sociality, but especially the latter, show us how another world is not only possible, but has been central to the vast portion of human history. At least the values and social practices can and must play such a role again.

One final point of some consequence. If Sahlins and others are correct, scarcity was not a fundamental human problem or conditioning feature for most of human history. The problem was, in fact, surplus. Bush people swam in a river of surplus that took the form of time to create a good life. In tributary and capitalist societies alike, real scarcity is created as a profound basis for the hoarding of wealth by the few. In tributary and capitalist societies, surpluses are at all costs kept from those who make them: spent on grandiose ego driven projects, conspicuous consumption and, very frequently, war. This while hunger and desperation provide the sting that drives work effort for the vast majority of people. Even as astute a thinker as Jean-Paul Sartre, in his *Critique of Dialectical Reason*, made of scarcity a transhistorical structure that conditioned human activity. The bush mode of production is a small, explosive epistemological device, planted under this deeply embedded ideological foundation. Perhaps George Bataille, a thinker who centred excess, deserves some attention in this regard.

11 Source Note

This chapter relies on the work of anthropologists who follow the main lines of argument laid down by Jean-Jacques Rousseau and Friedrich Engels. The work of Richard Lee, Marshall Sahlins and Stanley Diamond remains powerful and inspiring to us as leaders of a generational cohort of politicised anthropologists whose displacement in the field by theorists of 'hybridity' has had deeply unfortunate political consequences. The work of Eleanor Leacock deserves special attention among this cohort as a committed feminist whose work on gender relations among bush people places her in the pantheon of twentieth-century materialist feminists. Hugh Brody's work is particularly important in thinking about northern hunting cultures and points towards the contemporary implications for bush people of these sometimes-abstract arguments.

CHAPTER 5

Mode of Production and Materialist Cultural Politics

1 Introduction

When you walk down a trail, what you see depends upon what you know. If you know something about botany, you will notice unusual plants for this ecological zone, or the state of transition of the forest, or the presence or lack of plants indigenous to the area. If you know something of geology, you might step on and crush the rare orchid but notice the glacial striations in the rock, or a thin line in the middle of a quartz vein that seems promising – perhaps you rush back to town to start the process of staking a mineral claim. You can walk down the same trail as an artist, tripping over a gold vein and not thinking much of the rare cactus, but you find a place where the line of a ridge, the trees in the wind, the touch of sparkling colour in the pond just barely visible, all promise a lively landscape – you might spend an hour in that spot sketching or photographing or committing the scene to memory. The hunter might notice a flicker of a partridge tail off to the periphery of her vision, of a place where a moose bedded down for the night, or a rabbit trail calling out for a snare. The same walk, the same trail, for the lover perhaps leaves her stumbling over plants, partridges and rock veins, thinking only of the eyes of the one who waits eagerly for her return. What you see depends upon what you know. Cultures represent ways of seeing; they reveal and they occlude. Different ways of seeing open up vistas of knowledge and values: life choices. Perhaps the richest walk down the trail comes when we know a little bit about botany, a little bit about geology, a little bit about hunting, a little bit about art, a little bit about love. Mark Twain reputedly once said that to know less than two languages is to know none. The same can be said about culture.

Cultural difference is not particularly valued in the Marxist canon, which justifiably remains firmly attentive to the material conditions that might allow for a decent quality of life, an opportunity for every person to achieve their potential. Yet Marxism does provide the strongest analytical frame for thinking through cultural difference, and for negotiating cultural politics in a profoundly materialist way. The contemporary fashion for hybridity theory, a useful corrective to specious claims of cultural purity, circulated by political leaders desperate to distract attention from the avaricious structure of policies they underwrite, is not helpful in thinking about cultural difference, or even the cultural homogenisation that a totalising system ruthlessly advances. It is precisely at this point that the concept mode of production unlocks a door to understanding both historical change at a very broad level and cultural politics today in very specific national and international contexts.

In the Marxist canon, a mode of production consists of relations of production and forces of production, in large measure social organisation and technology. Marx's own descriptions of what he called 'precapitalist social formations', and Nicos Poulantzas's description of the spatial and temporal underpinnings of the modern nation, presume that modes of production produce and deploy quite different logics of space and time. These logics can be seen as a material precondition upon which expressive cultures and everyday life worlds are built. While Poulantzas's evocative description of capitalist space and time only and largely by implication suggests different spatial and temporal orders, Marx himself devoted some thought more directly to the way in which these logics are constructed and reconstructed. With Engels, he wrote powerfully and eloquently about the revolutionary transformations brought about by the bourgeoisie:

> The bourgeoisie cannot exist without constantly revolutionising the instruments of production, and thereby the relations of production, and with them the whole relations of society. Conservation of the old modes of production in unaltered form, was, on the contrary, the first condition of existence for all earlier industrial classes. Constant revolutionising of production, uninterrupted disturbance of all social conditions, everlasting uncertainty and agitation distinguish the bourgeois epoch from all earlier ones. All fixed, fast-frozen relations, with their train of ancient and venerable prejudices and opinions, are swept away, all new-formed ones become antiquated before they can ossify. All that is solid melts into air, all that is holy is profaned.[1]

Marx and Engels's famous passage from *The Communist Manifesto* is in effect commenting on the totalising restructuring of the material cultural platform upon which new ways of seeing and forms of everyday life were being reconstructed right before their eyes. A contemporary analytical description of this process has been offered by Fredric Jameson:

1 Marx 1974, p. 70.

> … the overtly 'transitional' moments of cultural revolution are themselves but the passage to the surface of a permanent process in human societies, of a permanent struggle between the various coexisting modes of production. The triumphant moment in which a new systemic dominant gains ascendancy is therefore only the diachronic manifestation of a constant struggle for the perpetuation and reproduction of its dominance, a struggle which must continue throughout its life course, accompanied at all moments by the systemic or structural antagonism of those older and newer modes of production that resist assimilation or seek deliverance from it. The task of cultural and social analysis thus construed within this final horizon will then clearly be the rewriting of its materials in such a way that this perpetual cultural revolution can be apprehended and read as the deeper and more permanent constitutive structure in which the empirical textual objects know intelligibility.[2]

Again, in very different language, this is pointing to the ongoing process of reshaping social life to meet the changing requirements of capital, which may draw on and exacerbate social divisions that remain as accretions from previous modes of production, or may just as eagerly sweep them away. And a key mechanism for these entrenchments and dissolutions are the unseen forms, such as the logic of time and space, that are everywhere naturalised.

To the idea that there is a spatial and temporal logic associated with each mode of production, we add that each mode of production involves also a way of knowing, a mode of subjectivity, and, perhaps, a form of language. A distinct logic of space, time, subjectivity, knowledge and language corresponds to each mode of production, allowing both the forces and relations of production the intelligibilities within which they develop; though, to be clear, these platforms or structures are designed as a result of the forces and relations of production and in turn condition the everyday life and expressive cultures that characterise social being. The following chapter will offer sketches of each mode of production attentive to these dimensions or logics, save for that of language. Neither of us is a linguist. We know that contemporary language use is a reconstruction and adaptation of older versions of the languages we now use, languages that come from the tributary mode of production. We have some sense of the distinctiveness of the languages associated with the bush mode of production. But we do not have the linguistics background that would be required to make any strong arguments on the issue, and leave the question to those in the appro-

2 Jameson 1983, p. 83.

priate fields of expertise. In what follows, then, we will examine the way each mode of production deploys a distinct logic of space, time, subjectivity and knowledge which act as a foundation for the expressive cultures and the quotidian routines of the generations of people who live within its boundaries.

The point of all of this is to show how expressive culture is built upon a platform that responds to the structural exigencies (or, in Marx's terms, presuppositions) of a particular mode of production. By discussing the three modes of production together an analysis can 'denaturalise' the normative dimensions of each of these socially produced underlying cultural features that characterise daily life: and this 'denaturalisation' is an essential gesture to imagining the other worlds that are possible. The implications for politics, particularly across colonial boundaries, can then be seen in materialist cultural terms. This is neither a new materialism nor an old culturalism, but an attempt to show some necessary intersections, and in particular how certain aspects of what is seen as culture have material affects, while certain material elements of life are deeply culturally inflected.

2 Spatial Logics I: Capitalism

For all the many volumes of studies and whole disciplines devoted to the issue, relatively little has said about the issue of spatial logic at the level of mode of production. Much work has been done around spatial use within capitalism, the tributary mode, and the bush mode of production that can be drawn upon, but paying attention at a sufficient level of abstraction to the similarities and differences has not been a robust theoretical concern. We will start with capitalism and work our way back through the tributary and bush modes, not nearly exhausting the topic but leaning on the lines of difference. Finally, though for analytical purposes we distinguish space and time; in fact, a spatial-temporal structure, or space-time, may be a critically useful tool: We prefer Sartre's concept of totalisation to Deleuze's evocative concept of territorialisation, for example, because the former affords thought into the manner in which processes of domination reshape, capture or invade both spheres of embodiment.

Capitalism relies on a spatial logic in which seriality, homogenisation, enclosure, rigid division, spectacle and surveillance are key elements, all involving and enacting a tendency towards abstraction. Most of these principles were developed in response to the needs of expanding factory production, and extend aspects of the spatial logic of factory production into the area of consumption and throughout everyday embodied practices. Seriality, the logic of the numerical sequence, is a social logic encountered on assembly lines or at the bakery (in production and consumption). It assists in the production of docility: The defining feature of a serial group is the fact that it does not define its own project. The logic of numerical sequence is so much a part of daily life it is normalised to the point of invisibility. Modernity's ethics is based in large measure on this simple principle of space-time: Who arrived in the space first has priority. There can be no discussion among participants of their particular embodied qualities that might lead to a rearrangement of the order of service. Only two principles override serial ethics: The wealthy have their own lanes, and the powerful will strip lands from those who may have occupied and used them first.

Homogenisation is also a governing spatial logic. Every airport in the world is the same. That is not an accident. The only difference involves what new spatial principle – new forms of signage, body conveyance, sense of newness itself – will originate wherever to become the next wave of a global assimilative logic. Spatial difference is beaten to a pulp, allowing for the creation of grids suitable for whatever purpose capital will need to design: an arena, a shopping mall, a super highway, an office building, a toxic wasteland. Texture and historicity are removed from public space, which becomes ever more banal and unendurable. The same line-up for the same burger is found, increasingly, in the remotest parts of the world. Capitalism desires a world of sameness upon which it can build, demolish, build anew, demolish anew, each time with a pale echo of some utopian promise: clean, modern, spacious, a place where nothing ever happens.

Enclosure remains a critical feature. Capital itself appears to need spatial containers, boundaries and borders within which it can play the game of 'inside-outside', obeying the inside rules when convenient, leaping or threatening to leap to the outside when there are super-profits to be had. The logic of boundaries remains compelling, whether in terms of national borders or in terms of internal gated communities. Bubbles of orderly wealth need to be maintained against the seething zombie multitudes scratching at the glass to get in. Border maintenance requires and demands policing organised to maintain the socially microscopic order of familial property as much as the socially macroscopic order of the nation state.

Space is also rigidly divided on class lines: The logics above apply to the broad mass of people and to the structure of the system as a whole. The very rich skip the lines, develop their idiosyncratic ocean front or penthouse paradises, and enclose themselves against the filthy masses. The gated, walled, enclosed enclave of the wealthy has always been an emblem of social hierarchy. The rich and the rest live in different worlds, and this has always been a constitutive feature of capitalist spatial logic, to such an extent that to be wealthy is almost entirely a matter of occupying spaces reserved for the exclusive few, and buying out of the logics that govern the rest. As to the rest, we know when we've crossed the invisible barrier of class, and hastily retreat with dignity intact to the sidewalk, where we belong.

The logic of spectacle is a spatial order that governs much of expressive cultural production. It is a social-spatial logic in which a small number of people engage in an action while a large number of people consume it with ears and eyes, as docile bodies. Although spectacle logic is easily associated with mass entertainment – musical concerts, sporting events, and the like – it is equally deployed in education (the class room), in politics (the rally, the televised speech), in spirituality (the sermon). Although the concept was developed by Guy Debord decades ago, in the contemporary moment spectacle logic is found in screen time that has overwhelmed space, time and sociality to an enormous degree. The concept is more pertinent than ever, because it embodies and naturalises the logic of social hierarchy: They, the geniuses, the talented, the deserving, get to be 'up there' and active while we, the dumb and poor, stay glued to our seats, if we're lucky enough to have a seat.

Surveillance involves a kind of reverse spectacle. Here, the knowledge that we are being watched, whenever, wherever, generates another level of docility. Again, the mechanisms of ensuring workers in productive environments do not steal diamonds or iPhones must be deployed in consumer environments to make sure buyers do not steal diamonds or iPhones. The proliferation of digital image capturing technologies has come to mean that our every public, and increasingly private, actions are recorded and vulnerable to police examination, should we dare to cross a line into any form of dissidence that threatens the private-property-based status quo.

The development of the market within the space of the emerging territorial state is fundamental to capitalist exchange relations. But the market does not develop autonomously. From beginning to end, it develops in tandem with the state and is dependent on it. Space and time take on a dialectical and dynamic quality under capitalism. Unequal development is its fundamental characteristic. An ongoing division between town and country, centre and hinterland, marks the accumulation of capital in the territorial state. The geographic layout of towns is formed by capitalist activity within them. The search for profit can induce capitalists arbitrarily to seize for development urban real estate at the expense of workers and the poor in a process which has been called accumulation by dispossession. Networks of towns develop in accord with a growing division of labour at the level of the national market. Unequal development within a state can include the development of capitalism at the expense of tributary and bush modes of production within them. The resultant contradictions may induce a process of combined and unequal development which can spur capitalist growth but also set off social convulsions and even revolution. Internationally unequal development expresses itself in the split between centre and periphery, as development at the centre is accompanied by the development of underdevelopment in the Global South. Capital is mobile, at times leaping over national boundaries, as it seeks new opportunities for profit in a process known as a spatial fix.

These logics are social-spatial and space-time logics, but they lean in the direction of space. The overall effect is to produce or encourage social docility, to entrench social hierarchy, and to create conditions conducive to capital accumulation. There are other elements of capitalist spatial logic – the concept of wilderness, the environment, the global, urbanisation – but they are second order logics in our view, worth attention in more specific contexts. These spatial logics are imbricated in contemporary technologies and the deeply hierarchical social relations that underwrite them.

3 Spatial Logics II: Tributary

The tributary mode of production involves a distinct set of spatial logics that are embodied, bounded, heterogenous, rural/local and expansive. The logic also supports social hierarchy or class distinction/differentiation. By embodied, we refer to the fact that space is organised according to its pre-given qualitative features: a sun-facing hill can perhaps be better for certain crops, a bend in the river can support a protective barrier. Features of the land are deployed to support activities – a place to build a village, a right of way, a pasture – and the land can be painstakingly adapted for productive or consumptive purposes: stepped terraces for rice growing, a clearing for a market. Primarily, the particular demands of agricultural production lead to a reshaping of landscapes, but a reshaping constrained or aided by the qualitative, particular features of the land in question.

The reshaping of land is partly conditioned by emerging property regimes associated with the tributary mode of production. This means that principles of drawing boundaries, marking limits, is a critical spatial feature. Lands in common, rights of way, sites of play and ceremony, become specific allowances that circulate around and through the emerging private property regimes. The fence, a technology perhaps developed for animal husbandry or containment, becomes a social tool to designate – make visible – property limits.

Land as a spatial logic is also heterogenous, with distinct types of spaces emerging in relation to social needs and qualities of the land itself. The forest as a site in contrast to the field, the urban in contrast to the more dominant rural, the sacred as opposed to the secular, are all special distinctions that may evolve from some complex interplay between social vision and pre-existing or constructed spatial qualities. Sites of rural production can become areas of specialised harvest or production and become associated with the qualities of particular agricultural products. Finally, space can be organised to reflect and enact social hierarchy: Built structures can be constructed to reflect, display and enact hierarchy, the division of spaces for social use can involve allocation of spaces with desired features (access to water or other resources, 'grand' views, and so on) to social elites.

The distinction between rural and urban space develops in these spatial contexts. Urban space in early years may develop in a largely unplanned or organic fashion, though in later periods of the tributary mode of production deliberate organisation of urban spaces (for example, the north-south axis and grid-like organisation of ancient Chinese cities), particularly around institutionalised spiritual demands, takes greater prominence. In later periods of tributary city-states, the distinction between urban and rural life grows sharper.

Population growth is a feature of the tributary mode of production which leads towards the need for increasing land. As a result of this and other factors – for example, the development of what today is called 'toxic masculinity', associated with the need to facilitate intergenerational transfers of property, which leads to a 'warrior'-oriented social interest – the spatial logic relies on expansion: cutting forests, conquering lands nearer or further, setting up colonies, and so on. The 'spread' of what calls itself 'civilisation' is a critical feature of the spatial logic in tributary modes of production.

We argue that pastoralists are also to be considered within the tributary mode of production. This is because of the deeply entrenched notion of social hierarchies embedded in pastoral social forms. However, while pastoral spatial logics involve all the principles enumerated above, they appear differently within the expressive culture. As well, nomadism, when attached to population growth and patriarchy, gives a much more powerful push behind the expansive element of tributary forms. Hence the 'war machine' element of many nomadic pastoralist societies when they pass particular population thresholds.

4 Spatial Logics III: Bush

While the bush mode of production shares some features with the tributary mode, the social context and productive demands give these features an entirely different logical orientation. Spatial logic among bush people is embodied, rural, heterogenous, territorial and nomadic. The social and spiritual logic emphasises community-based circles of people. In this case, embodied again means that the qualitative features of the land are intimately known and deployed. Although there may be deliberate attempts to reshape land (from more or less extensive use of fire through to constructing weirs, buffalo jumps, or other smaller-scale productive improvements), this tends to be less pervasive and to operate within the ecological forms of the territory involved (promoting some kinds of indigenous plant growth over others, for example). The forest, plain, tundra, outback, jungle, ocean and subarctic bush itself are all ecological zones whose productive resources can replenish themselves when used by local gathering, hunting and fishing peoples.

This is also a rural form of spatial logic, but in a dramatically distinct fashion, inasmuch as there is no significant urban space to be contrasted with. While temporary gatherings of significant size might seasonally take place, the sites of such gatherings tend towards the temporary and deploy organic spatial forms. Permanent trading communities – such as the Mandan villages at the big bend of the Mississippi River in early historic North America – of some size did exist, and both Haudenosaunee and Northwest Coast bush people built semi-permanent villages, because these were places conducive to agriculture, trade or continual coastal based harvesting. Even then, in population terms such villages were comparatively small. The broader point is that many, and likely most, bush people may never have seen a permanent urban space or gathering larger than a few thousand people at most. That the spatial logic can even be called rural is, in some respects, a retrospective nominalism, coming from the current analytical space in which the urban not only exists but dominates social life.

The heterogenous logic of space in the case of the bush mode of production refers to the fact that the different features of the ecological territory are understood and used with deep knowledge of and respect for such differences. A 'good' site for a fish camp, or caribou hunt, or nut gathering all involve different specific productive activities closely tied to the features of specific spaces. Sacred or spiritual sites can also be found through the bush, as well as places where medicines can be found. The land is not uniform: The qualitative nature of space may be closely tied to the different kinds of practices that will take place.

The tendency of bush spatial logics is to be both territorial and nomadic; the two are distinct but interrelated. In much of the world, bush people made or make seasonal use of resources within a more or less closely defined territory. Some territories were used and occupied by one distinct group, nation, band or tribe; in other cases portions of land may have been shared or used by different social groups in different seasons. The territory was a site of nomadic travel, not 'randomly wandering the earth' mythic nomadism, but using the seasonal ecological resources within a defined territory. For example, in the Arctic, Inuit may have fished in the spring, hunted seals or whale in the open water season of summer, trekked inland in the fall to hunt caribou (for winter clothing), and moved out onto the sea ice for seal hunting in the winter. Sometimes these involved population concentrations and dispersals: Spring or summer fishing or whale hunting camps might have involved a few hundred or even a thousand people, who would then disperse for much smaller trapping or hunting camps in the late fall or winter.

Such nomadic movements had profound impacts on social life. Egalitarianism in material wealth could prevail because in this context moveable property was literally a burden. Accumulation had a very immediate limit: whatever one and one's few beasts of burden could carry. Objects themselves might be viewed with something like suspicion rather than the desiring relation naturalised in modern times: One first sees any object literally as a burden. The nomadism of bush people curtailed desire for accumulation of things, contributing to the overall egalitarian ethos socially as well as to the possibility of generalised affluence.

5 Temporal Logics I: Capitalism

Temporality in capitalism also closely mirrors the demands of productive activity and the social hierarchies that surround and found the activities. Again, the logic moves towards abstraction: Time is homogenised, serial, inflexible, and progressive. At this or any moment we can be aware of the exact time in the most far-flung part of the world. Clock and calendar temporality have been universalised under capitalism, so that regardless of political or cultural differences, exchange can be rationally managed. There is one time and one form of time, imposed against determined resistances first upon a growing cohort of factory and field labourers in their productive lives, and ultimately globally, in the sense of ruling all aspects of life and in the sense of coming to dominate nearly every corner of the world. While certain elements of time remain subservient to qualitative exigencies – the seasons, the annual circuit around the sun, the daily rotation of the earth – all of these are brought to heel through numerical abstraction. One day leads to the next, one year to the next: All can be regulated, counted, and sit comfortably in a homogenised, nearly universal logic.

The clock and calendar institute and enact the logic of seriality in time. Time rigidly follows the logic of numerical sequence. This allows it to be counted, measured, accumulated, bought, sold and managed. Bodies and relations must move around the exigencies of serial time. Learning and working, celebrating and mourning, resting and exercising, praying and loving, all activities find their time within and usually constrained by the serial structure of temporality. Each productive or leisure activity can be clearly delineated in serial temporal terms – from the one-hour lunch break to the final deadline of the report. All bodies, all attention spans, all abilities, must conform to this serial temporal logic, which, again, is also a fundamental of capitalist systemic ethics: How much time measured numerically do I give to this task, this relation, this sleep?

This form of time is surprisingly inflexible. The clocks only move one way, so too the calendars. If, heaven forfend, the football (whatever football) season is interrupted, however will so many comparative measurements of player and team skill be made? Debt, a critical element in the overall economic mechanism of ensuring social control, is calculated according to time: How long will it take to pay off the student loan, the mortgage, the credit card, the same day emergency loan? The fixity of time is a critical underlying structure of capital accumulation: Capital's managers must know with precision that thirty years hence the same logic will be operative.

Temporality is also progressive in that the logic of capital accumulation means that growth is demanded. Time cannot simply repeat – it must march along the triumphal procession of growth. The ideology of progress itself is not unrelated to this: Every day in every way the world gets better and better. This mantra may actually be relevant only to the very rich, all the more reason for it to be sold to everyone else. The 'times' improve along an abstract, linear, serial, accumulative, inflexible, universal logic designed precisely to ever and always insist on such improvement.

Time is also embodied along the lines of social hierarchy: The wealthier one is, the less one is forced to watch the clock. The balance of work/leisure rests heavily on the former for the poor, and the latter for the rich. The jobless do drop out of aspects of serial temporality for greater or shorter periods, but constant worry, food insecurity, housing precarity, and social debasement are the close companions of this: Calling it leisure is as toxic a lie as calling the Sackler family philanthropists. The social world can be seen in terms of those who 'have' time, those who do not, and those kept marginal as a disciplinary warning to the latter.

Turnover time, being fundamental to profitability, there is a basic tendency towards the compression of space and time, as speed is of the essence. Time is no longer seen to move in cycles but rather progressively, the future always being defined as being better than the past. But this sense of progressive development also gives rise to a sense of history which fundamentally emerges from the progressive accumulation of capital. Time has different speeds. There are long periods where the cycles of production and the economic are primary. But then there are moments of crises and revolution where politics are most important and even crucial. Capitalism is repeatedly marked by such revolutions. It is as a result important to understand that the political texts of Marx are as valuable as *Capital* itself for understanding the politics of a particular historical conjuncture.

6 Temporal Logic II: Tributary

The temporal logic of the tributary mode of production is organised around, in the first instance, the demands of agricultural or pastoral productive activities, and, secondarily, around the two interrelated poles of social hierarchy embodied in religious and political institutions. In contrast to capitalism, the logic is cyclical, spiritual, fractured and local. These logics work in the direction of embodiment rather than abstraction. Obviously, both the spatial and temporal logic of nomadic pastoral communities is quite different from settled agricultural communities, but there are important features in common as well.

Time among tributary peoples is cyclical, oriented in its pores towards the changing seasons. On the immediate or everyday level, the seasonal time of year entirely inflects the activities and practices of both the peasant, and, although in different ways, the aristocrats and high priests. As these periods and practices repeat, they instantiate a rhythmic notion of temporality, cycles of activity, generations, ceremonies, dynasties great and small. Priestly activities may be organised around the demands of changing seasons, with ritual life aimed at ensuring rain or abundance. The day and the season are the two key cyclical temporal units. Although there is a logic of saving and accumulation, it is dominated by the logic of repetition. Over generations a familial holding may grow or shrink. The accumulation of food storage techniques and technologies is critical to the long-term success of any village or region. However, these forms of accumulation run against the current of a temporal logic that emphasises repetition. The time in labour or in products that are 'owed' by the serf to the local or distant aristocrat is roughly measured in days or tasks to be completed.

The institutionalisation of spirituality is a form of abstraction practiced by tributary societies. Gods and priests alike are organised into a social hierarchy that reflects the earthly forms of social stratification. Time therefore also has a spiritual dimension, articulated through ceremonial life. Bells, songs, or other forms of noise wrought for spiritual purposes might mark the daily rhythm, while rituals associated with life events – funerals, marriages, births – might interrupt or punctuate those rhythms. Sacred time may involve passive observation of greater or lesser scales of spectacle: sitting quietly while the priest reads from the sacred books or gaining a good prospect from which to watch and witness the sacrifice. As well, village carnivals often involve inversions of both the social and the sacred order, rupturing time with the shock of defamiliarisation contained only by the fact that the daily rhythm will return.

Time is fractured in tributary societies. Each new dynasty installs its own 'year one'. Each distinct region, under sway of a different dynastic familial network, marks its own sequence of years. These may barely make a noticeable change to the peasants, or may involve dramatic swings, usually for the worse, in what local hegemons charge in tribute or tax. There is no universal or homogenous time but rather a quilt of distinct recorded or unrecorded temporal systems. To travel to a distant part of the world is to slowly travel across a temporal fracture, into a temporal zone only partially commensurable with that of home.

There is, consequently, a local dimension to time. Each village or complex of villages may have its/their own particular holidays and feast days, common task days, sense of what marks the change of seasons in their particular locale, notion of intergenerational obligation or right, or other temporal notion within the broad general logic. Meanwhile, we can be sure that the wealthy will be hunting, enumerating their collected or owed tributes, playing more or less elaborate games, manoeuvring to have dalliances with each other, or pontificating in the councils of war: living a very different mix of practices at the same time as their immiserated 'subjects'.

7 Temporal Logic III: Bush

The bush runs on a whole other temporal flow. In contrast to the other modes of production, in the bush, time is activity-focused, repetitive, spiritual, more deeply embodied (personal), and oscillates between condensed and unspooled temporal modes. Temporality is even more fractured in the bush mode: Each familial hunting group makes its own daily decisions about what to do and where to be within the frame of a particular ecological niche, and therefore lives its own time. Seasonal gatherings take place according to the rhythms of the land: after spring melt at a large fishing camp, or before a large buffalo hunt, for example.

The activity-focused structure of time applies to productive, leisure and spiritual practices. Each will consume the amount of time needed to complete the task, whether practical or ceremonial or recreational. A story will be told in the time it demands. A deer can be hunted over the course of an hour or several days. A ceremony can continue until all participants, exhausted, have had their needs met. A canoe can be built intensively in several days, or over the course of a month in the gaps that intersperse other activities. Time operates under the command of practice, rather than the reverse.

The logic of repetition is, in the bush, even more forceful than in the fields: In the latter, it is tempered somewhat by a drive to accumulate. In the bush, where really only knowledge accumulates, repetition becomes an even stronger logic. One looks for the character of the departed in the actions of children: Reincarnation theories have a stronger hold in the bush than in the fields or cities. One aims to embody the character of one's ancestors: Tradition here is strongly personalised. Repetition in formal rhetoric or high speech is a mirror of this, as is the extraordinary mimetic ability (or faculty) that can be found among bush people. People are driven not by the desire for more, but by the desire to live the good life that their parents and grandparents enjoyed.

Bush people produce a spirituality that does not tend to take institutional forms, but is personally chosen within a pattern. The pattern reflects egalitarian social forms which determine that ceremonies take place in (literal) circles, for example. But the length of a woman's seclusion ceremony or hallucinogenic journey in temporal terms depends upon the body and will of the practitioner, or the accidents of whatever external events may intrude or be welcomed within the spiritual time. Spiritual time is less demarked, and more a part of everyday life, where expressions of gratitude for game, for relationships, for water, for life itself, can take a wide variety of forms and can burst out of any moment. It can be said that there is no boundary between secular and spiritual within the bush mode: Though specific ceremonies may mark life stages or other events or needs, there is a daily presence of the spiritual as well.

The time-logic of bush people is deeply personal. Each individual and family has its own rhythms and each body obeys its own temporal logic. Some are slower, some are more energetic, some are more contented: Each has their own reason to wake or sleep or nap or work or play according to when they are in the extended 'leisure' time or the oscillation of work and play/rest/leisure that daily life operates within. The time of the body is more truly followed among bush people than among any others. Such a temporal logic is incomprehensible to those within capitalist and tributary modes alike where the demands of production insistently override the nuances of the body.

Finally, there is an oscillation of temporalities, from condensed moments of action (spearing the seal) to extended periods of patient waiting, among hunters and fishers, at least. Work done at the hearth or in gathering tends more towards unspooled time, leisurely, slow and steady activities of fundamental importance to group well-being. But time can condense in both the camp and the hunting or fishing grounds: A dissatisfaction bursts into the open in an eruptive social conflict; a herd is frightened by a small group towards the main hunting party. Unspooled time is the daily norm, but moments of intensity are common enough that everyone is prepared for them. The form of time associated with waiting – at the seal hole where a seal may or may not show up after many, many hours, on the plains where a change in wind direction may bring the buffalo one's scent, in the mountains where the thin line of small white dots in the high distance mark the return of sheep to accessible grounds before the onset of winter – is perhaps the most distinct, greatest marker of temporal alterity, not the miserable wait for the late train or doctor when so much else needs to be done, but the waiting in which the drift of time and consciousness synchronise, when work and leisure collapse into each other, when the body is at rest but poised and thought holds an attentive element of focus even in distraction, daydream and concerted or creative problem solving.

All of this rests in part on the extended notions of respect for personal autonomy that socially grounds the egalitarianism of bush people. Every person has a base right to respect, which means their experience and articulation of temporality remains in their own control. This is a specific form of what Marx saw as meaningful freedom. While disjunctured and incommensurable, the time of this freedom is perhaps the most precious of human resources.

8 The Logic of Subjectivity across Three Modes of Production

The way in which 'self' is understood and the manner in which the 'individual' and the 'community' is defined are complex processes that shift dramatically across the distinct modes of production. This deserves attention as it is also a material platform upon which quotidian practice, expressive culture, legal foundation and the overall ideological temperament of a way of life is built. Each mode of production forecloses and opens options of individual self-understanding and relational engagements. These are directly related, as are all the elements discussed in the chapter, in the manner of presuppositions to expressive culture and everyday life established by the productive forces and relations. The description that follows is, again, meant to highlight critical aspects and will be even briefer than the preceding discussions of space and time.

Capitalism emphasises the possessive individual and works explicitly in its primitive accumulation phase and ongoing movement to destroy meaningful communities. In this circumstance, the individual is the site or locus of extraordinary lines of force, and is treated as a member of a serial collectivity wherein she or he is expected to compete for material wealth and social status. Although the individual is raised to a pinnacle of social standing, everywhere individuation and character are actually homogenised to an unprecedented degree. National, racialised and gendered distinctions, as well as distinctions related to sexual self-definition and orientation, and distinctions related to embodied abilities, are all deployed in specific capitalist contexts to set people apart from each other or to mobilise scapegoating mechanisms that deflect outrage over a basic failure to deliver anything approximating a good life. Generalised narcissism is structurally promoted by this social structure, as is envy and ressentiment. The state invades the interiority of the subject, offering legal positionings of the self that either establish docility or narrowly sanctioned and alienated forms of social and political agency, as well as ensuring self-policing. Collective and particularly class agency or solidarity are repressed in ideological (historical and contemporary) accounts and in practice. Most people are trained to believe they are equal to all and members of a massive middle class, yet people are also socially trained in recognising social hierarchy everywhere around them and deferring to it, particularly in the work place but also as a feature of everyday culture.

Explicit deference to social hierarchy is a cultural feature of the tributary mode of production, which institutionalises spirituality in a manner that provides sweeping justification to deep social inequality. However, the demands of production promote intergenerational communities with close attachments to specific places. Patriarchy is a structural feature that develops in large part to ensure intergenerational passage of property, especially land, though it is of a piece with the development of social hierarchy itself. Deference, humility and community feeling among the peasant classes contrast with arrogance and self-interest among the secular and spiritual aristocrats. Religious difference and commonality are key features of social life. Participation in ceremony paradoxically builds communal bonds while strengthening social hierarchy. Millenarian and revolutionary movements emerge in these contexts when the predations of the rulers make the lives of tillers untenable.

The bush mode of production involves deep intergenerational community bonds and a striking individualism. Respect for the autonomy of the other is an ethical ground of subjectivity, which allows for the demand of respect for the self. A gendered division of labour is common but exists in a context of gender egalitarianism. Character has significant meaning in this context, and a wide range of social difference can be tolerated and indeed embraced. Familial bonds are important, but extra-familial social elements (such as clans, forms of nominalism, work partners) work to build important social ties outside of the family. Attachment to territory or to specific places can be a critical feature of how the self is defined. Kulchyski discovered after years of research that asking Inuit elders when they were born often produced a shrug or vague response; ask where they were born and they could often respond in detail, with some showing the exact few feet in a remote hunting camp where they had come into the world.

Egalitarianism in practice among bush people involves the establishment of much more complex social structures, and individual capabilities within those structures, than the hierarchies of tributary and capitalist modes. Hierarchy as a structure allows subjects a simple way of defining rights and obligations: We owe to those above us on the hierarchy and have commands for those below us. As hierarchy grows more prevalent, and inequality is exacerbated, the structure gains more gradations and becomes even simpler: Subjects will rarely encounter someone they cannot place instantly and determine their degree of deference to or arrogance towards. The constant attentiveness to individual material gain and social advancement become the most common and simplest motivations for social practice: Everyone attempts to socialise upwards. This is particularly true of capitalism though elements are present in tributary societies as well. The bush mode demands each individual 'size up' every other and build bonds or enmities based on the character of the other, a much more complex task demanding much greater flexibility and attentiveness.

The construction of subjectivity is always a dialectical process involving a dynamic between how the society and state position a specific subject and how the subjects draw from their circumstances, relations and personal histories to position themselves. The individuals who form a part of a serial collective are ready for the assembly line; the individuals who know their divinely ordained lot in life are ready for work in the field; the individuals whose character is formed among respecting peers and wise elders is ready to contribute to the hearth or hunt and to stand together in strength and contentment on the earth. Upon these foundations, mountains of cultural objects and forms, and of ideological containers, are constructed.

9 Ways of Knowing

'How do we know what we know?' is the question asked by epistemology. In our work, epistemology itself is transected or ordered by modes of production. Each mode of production develops systems of knowledge which get built upon during the course of a particular social formation's history. Knowledge can operate according to a logic of repetition or according to a logic of accumulation. Knowledge can be tied to embodied practice (experience) of the knowledge holder, or be produced through logical processes of abstraction. Knowledge can be situated and contextual, or universal and, again, abstracted from the specific site of its production or from any specific site. Knowledge is required both as an aid to production and as a foundation of personal contentment or dissatisfaction. Knowledge is, finally, another foundation or platform of culture presupposed by the productive demands of each mode of production and therefore distinct across the modes.

The development of capitalism brings with it a dramatic change in knowledge production, marked by the enlightenment and the equation of science with truth. Instrumental reason forms the main line of knowledge production, though speculative philosophy can also play its part. The form of knowledge becomes entirely secularised, though it inherits a whole baggage of habits formed by tributary societies and the institutionalised spiritualities (religions) that it both builds from and profoundly challenges. Knowledge production is invested in this context in the domination of the natural world, a natural world it itself defines. Universalism and abstraction are key underlying principles to knowledge production. The university and research institute become the secular institutional embodiments of knowledge production; scholasticism largely gives way to the laboratory in the former and is entirely exhaustive of the latter. Knowledge is parceled and differentiated into highly specialised fields of study; it is recorded in a variety of forms to ensure it can be exchanged or distributed intergenerationally; it is increasingly subject to the laws of private property through intellectual property rights. The form of knowledge is an enormously self-confident instrumental reason, and ascribes to itself wisdom and ethics, though either is to be found rather as a rare accident than a structural feature. New knowledge is prized – is the prize *par excellence*! – as it is an actual or potential source of capital accumulation. Knowledge is therefore bound to accumulation, itself accumulates, and therefore produces an ideological justification based on the notion of an endless progress marked by endless accumulation of knowledge.

Since the institutionalisation of spirituality through religion plays such a dominant part in the tributary mode of production, knowledge is closely tied to it and indeed is developed and expressed through the form of religious language. Secular knowledge can contradict sacred knowledge only at great peril if at all. Empirical observation gives way here to scholasticism, by which is meant the close reading of sacred texts. Sacred knowledge is the basis of moral codes and does have a direct concern with ethics, though the moral codes almost exhaust themselves in the defense of hierarchy. Knowledge founded on practice does increase over long durations, though setbacks and losses also occur. At the village level, narrative knowledge – stories of near and far places, stories from the past – holds sway. But a very close reading of the land or domesticated animals allows peasant producers an intimate, empirically based degree of knowing, tied to the demands of productivity. As long as this knowing conforms to the parameters established by faith, it is permitted. Knowledge held by women as healers, midwives or land-based spiritualists is often challenged by deeply patriarchal religious leaders, who may prove determined to repress unorthodox ways of knowing that challenge aspects of the hegemonic religious belief. But subcultural and unorthodox knowledges do sometimes flourish: Many major religions that developed in the late phases of the tributary mode – Judaism, Bhuddism, Christianity, Hinduism, Taoism, Islam – started as challenges to the religious status quo. Religion gives the original license allowing knowledge to act as the main instrument for the domination of nature.

In the bush, knowledge frequently takes a narrative form, is personal (tied to individual embodied practice: that is, experiential) and often empirical, based on observation. Knowledge is transmitted across many generations, and grows and deepens over long periods of time. Repetition is a more primary setting of knowledge than accumulation. Hunters are very close observers of animals and each hunter develops a personal knowledge base. Relationality ethically steeps knowledge, so that 'nature' is not understood to be dominated, but rather understood to be an interdependent source of a good life, and itself alive. Social knowledge, particularly related to ethics, are codified to a small degree and disseminated through stories, which may be mythic or may be based on events undergone or witnessed by the teller. Knowledge can be incommensurable from one person to the next, be fragmentary and/or may be related to a holistic vision or sensibility. In a context of widespread respect for personal autonomy, each person has their own 'truth', their own story, their own inflection of the spiritual or life way. Even where these may contradict as they often do, they can peacefully co-exist.

10 Conclusion

Each of these intersecting areas or matrices is a platform, an underlying material structure upon which daily life and expressive culture builds. Time and space, subjectivity and knowledge, all have a form predicated on the structural demands and limitations established by social relations and technological capacities. The forms of these elements themselves presuppose those relations and capacities. How a daily action or a cultural symbol become expressed are limited and enabled by these platforms. In general, it is possible to build a narrative, across the modes, of increasing abstraction, universalism and homogeneity as one moves from the bush to the field to the factory/office. However, we reject the notion that this narrative is 'progressive' in any way, inasmuch particularly as these features in no way imply an advance in quality of life or in ethical behaviour. In fact, by those latter standards the narrative could well operate in reverse. Progressive change does happen over longer or shorter durations within modes of production: Bush people of the *Caaguasu* have not used the same technologies or techniques since their first arrival, but deepened and broadened their knowledge and approaches over centuries. Farmers in Africa likewise were able to invent or borrow practices and tools and incorporate them over long periods. The pace of change in capitalism hardly needs comment and determines that each generation will leave behind a very different world than the one it came into.

Two elements of the capitalist mode of production have been left out of the foregoing account, but also inflect the cultural platforms enumerated above. These are, firstly, the fact that the commodity form applies to these; space and time, subjectivity and knowledge may all be commodified: Space is the easiest place to see this as land has long been subject to the laws of exchange value, but time is also bought and sold particularly through the entertainment industries but more far-reachingly as the abstraction that grounds value. As is subjectivity in which a good deal of material is required to express a self-forged 'identity', and as is knowledge which increasingly is confined by the laws of property.

The second element to be foregrounded here is that the capitalist mode of production is totalising on a level previously unseen in history. While the first Qin emperor attempted to establish conformity in weights and measures and road widths and other areas, he was constrained by the limits of his political control, as was every other hegemon before and after who wished to homogenise the world in their image during their particular tributary dynastic reign. Capitalist totalisation has spread over time and place, not limited by the boundaries of this or that leader or even national system. Resistance to that totalisation is one of the key largely unnamed social struggles of the contemporary world, and will be a key concern in the pages that follow.

11 Source Note

A starting point for this discussion is Nicos Poulantzas's chapter on 'The Nation' in his *State, Power, Socialism*. Fredric Jameson and David Harvey's distinct but related writings on postmodernism develop theories of spatiality, while E.P. Thompson's essay on time and work discipline in his book on *Customs in Common* is a *tour de force* on that subject.

CHAPTER 6

Mode of Production Now

The historical development of capitalist modernism itself may have been given some propulsion as an effect of plague/pandemic-induced depopulations in the fourteenth century, which created conditions for a restless peasantry to demand more for their subsistence. We write in the historic shadow of a world pandemic. And so we find it necessary to insist that an externally induced catastrophe on its own is not a sufficient cause of structural change at the level of mode of production, in spite of the many historical accounts that would prefer such narrative digressions. Rather, social conditions may reach of dramatic peak of conflict – usually related to increases in stark inequalities – which then allows a seemingly contingent, accidental event to help ignite the tinder of revolution. The coronavirus in and of itself may not be cause of change, but has ravaged a world already viciously riven by a deeply entrenched, brutal and increasing inequality. The effects of that inequality are becoming more visible as the pandemic itself exacerbates it: We now know, if we didn't before, that the needs of capital for growth (called 'the economy') are everywhere more important than human life. The re-election of Trump and his dismantling of the U.S. government represents in part the latest desperate attempt of capital to exacerbate and prolong the massive overreach of the wealthy by removing the last tepid state-imposed barriers to their unquenchable need for more.

1 Capitalist Crises and Socialist Possibilities

The crisis of the capitalist mode is as general as was the late mediaeval European crisis. The pandemic itself was set off by the encroachment of capitalist development (in China) into the deepest reaches of the environment. A metabolic relationship between society and nature is a feature of both the bush and tributary mode. From its beginnings, capitalism undermined this more balanced form of relationship. Under capitalism, nature became simply a free storehouse, an obstacle or a dumping ground. The chickens have come home to roost in the twenty-first century in the form of the growing spread of lethal viruses (now ironically among chickens!), the build-up of carbon dioxide, global warming, the melting of the polar ice caps, desiccation and deforestation, the depletion of species including food stocks and the poisoning of the water and the air. Under capitalism, life, including human life, is increasingly unsustainable.

Economically capitalism has entered a zombie state, a state of the living dead. Profits have been sliding downwards since the 1970s, growing instability punctuated by outright collapses in 2000–1, 2008 and 2020. The realm of finance – the last rampart of capitalism – is more and more divorced from that of productive investment which is moribund. Whereas an arms-length relationship between the market and the state has always been a tenet of capitalism and a dogma of neoliberalism, businesses are now permanently dependent on government subsidies and the jobs and incomes of workers dependent on the state. In the current moment, the criminals have been empowered to seize the state entirely. There is zero possibility that this state of affairs can be reversed within the logic of an existing system in which the needs of capital are paramount, the needs of people secondary.

Social inequality in the advanced capitalist countries has reached levels not seen since the nineteenth century or during the *Ancien Régime*. Inequality of this scale is both economically and socially destabilising. And we are not even referring to Latin America, the Middle East and India and Pakistan. This is the context for the outbreak of the Black Lives Matter protests which have spread from the United States to Canada and Europe. It is very significant that in the United States and elsewhere white working-class people, especially young people, have joined these protests. Racism may have less and less power to trump class hatred, even as it is pumped up by the cheerleaders of capitalism. Indeed, we are seeing the welling up of class struggle worldwide and notably in places as diverse as France, Bolivia and Lebanon.

The opening decades of this century have seen the emergence of China as a threat to the global hegemony of the United States, itself the last and greatest of the imperialist powers. With a population four times greater than the United States and a level of education, skill and political understanding which overshadows it, its New Silk Road is likely to annul the historic ascendancy of the Western capitalist states and restore the dominance of Eurasia in global affairs as during the tributary period. In the meantime, this centaur-like state – head socialist, body capitalist – is now locked in an inter-imperialist struggle with the United States marked by tariff walls and growing war preparations which include rising military expenditures. Protectionism and border restrictions have become a global phenomenon. It is important to underscore that it is the United States, increasingly on the defensive economically and politically, which is primarily responsible for this situation as it tries to protect its eroding hegemony. But this recrudescence of imperialist rivalry flies in the face of capitalism's urgent need for freer trade and investment opportunities and constitutes another symptom of capitalist crisis.

The final symptom of the crisis of the capitalist mode is the collapse of the neoliberal ideology and in fact the growing questioning of liberalism, representative democracy and the political and intellectual elites that control it. It is symptomatic that this questioning is most apparent in the United States, the heartland of capitalism. But it is apparent in all the advanced capitalist states and elsewhere, where the growing attraction of socialism, but also fascism, is reawakening.

What would a new socialist mode of production look like? We should begin by looking at what Marx and Engels thought. It is commonly suggested that Marx and Engels had little to say about socialism because they thought that the new mode would define itself through revolutionary historical changes and not through wishful thinking. Through reading certain passages of the *Grundrisse*, or examining a mirror image of the description of estranged labour from the *1844 Manuscripts*, it is possible to tease out some very strong ideas. But we turn to the work of Paresh Chattopadhyay, who by careful study of their texts has demonstrated that, in fact, they had a lot to say about the socialist mode. Or rather, the socialist/communist mode as they thought of the two terms as synonymous. The following observations are therefore based on Professor Chattopadhyay's analysis to which is added our commentary.

It is out of capitalism and only capitalism that the new mode can develop. It is capitalism which creates the degree of material wealth and the socialisation of labour and production necessary to socialism. Without a sufficient material foundation and necessary degree of economic interdependence, antagonism and coercion will sooner or later weaken and undermine the free and willing cooperation required under socialism. Moreover, in this globalised world with its ecological and health problems and already existing levels of economic interdependence, cooperation and coordination at the international level is indispensable. The socialist mode of production will be international although its exact form is unknown. It is possible that the notion of federation borrowed by the United States and Canada from Haudenosaunee peoples could play a role in a better global order. The forces of production have developed to the point that a new global political order is absolutely required. Those forces have also produced newer means of global communication that allow for ethics to truly be embodied on a global level, a prerequisite for the necessary internationalism to come. The barriers to world commerce which are growing are not the only reason for the world economic crisis but they are important to it. Moreover, these economic frictions are deepening international political and military conflicts.

A new global political order is furthermore required because the fundamental legacy left by capitalism is not simply inequality based on class in every state, but uneven development between states. This unevenness is the source not only of poverty but also imperialism. The establishment of socialism entails a new global political order. The absence of such an order is a major reason behind the current economic depression and the anarchy of imperialist rivalry. As things stand, the forces of production are in complete contradiction with the relations of production. Not least of the contradictions is the fact that reducing population size, a secondary response to growing ecological crises, would be anathema to processes of capital accumulation which need continued growth in spite of the fact that the world is finite. Contradiction after contradiction has developed – the environmental crisis, pandemic, vast inequality and social unrest, economic crisis, erosion of public trust in the established political order, and mounting international tensions. Striking is the fact that, despite the many differences in the circumstances of each of the multitude of nation states, there is a growing convergence in the character of problems and conflicts. It can also be noted that environmental struggles, often on the territories of bush people, have gained greater prominence, and directly confront the logic of unlimited accumulation essential to the regime of capital. Given the multiplicity and seriousness of these contradictions, the possibilities of reform amid a renewed surge of capitalist growth and profitability are unlikely. Phantasms like crypto-currency will not save the day for capital (unless as may be possible there is in fact a liquidity crises), but rather until it collapses serve as a vehicle for the increasing criminality of the whole capitalist class. Abstracting from these contradictions, one arrives at the ultimate contradiction which encapsulates all the rest, that between the proletariat – the greatest force of production of them all – and the capitalist class.

This working class, which constitutes more and more of humanity, shows increasing signs of becoming class-conscious and ripe for revolution. In order for this class to carry through a revolution, it must organise itself to overcome the bourgeoisie. The latter controls money and the means of production, the state apparatus, including the police and military and the principal media. Moreover, it has long experience at governing, including safeguarding private property, suppressing the working class and dividing the working class through the scapegoating of some element within it. Therefore, the proletariat needs to develop its own institutions and media and, above all, a revolutionary party capable of overcoming the opposition to it. The exact form that such a party should take is unclear. It should be as broad-based and democratic as possible, allowing for many different opinions and tendencies which reflect the diversity of the left. Its leadership should be accountable to the base. At the same time, its members should be bound to implement decisions of the party democratically arrived at. Clearly, the party needs to develop a military capacity to overcome the monopoly of force exercised by the bourgeois state. The degree of violence required for success in a revolutionary situation is inversely proportional to the level of popular support the revolution enjoys, and in particular its alliances with other popular organisations and social groups. Seizure of the commanding heights of capitalism or, in other words, the means of production and the state institutions in advanced capitalist countries is key to the overthrow of the capitalist system as an international system. This was the original goal of the October Revolution and it remains the strategic goal of socialist revolution. The Trumpian dismantling of the U.S. constitutional order, with a notable acquiescence on the part of the Democratic Party there, illustrates that with enough will the old order can be dismantled quite quickly. The left must show this degree of determination. In this moment, characterised in part by a rising tide of fascism, we refuse to give into despair and turn our attention to the practicality of ushering in a better world.

Such a revolution would be an act of self-emancipation. It would be experienced as a liberation from bourgeois control of the means of production through the state. These would now be in the hands of the mass of workers. One can only imagine the euphoria attendant on such an event. But this revolution which destroys the bourgeois state and socialises the means of production initiates a prolonged transition to socialism by means of the dictatorship of the proletariat, which ends with the abolition of the working class itself. The dictatorship of the proletariat is essential to establishing the socialist mode of production. As the workers initially do not control means of production in the way that landlords or bourgeois did, then political control through the dictatorship of the proletariat is the only means by which it can establish its rule. This period might have its coercive aspects in the same way as the bourgeois dictatorship can be coercive. But as socialism entrenches itself its coercive aspects lessen. Indeed, the state itself begins to decline and the workers lose their characteristics as a class as class-based society disappears. In this context, the elements of socialist values to be found among certain peasant cultures and bush peoples can flourish and can provide material social examples of communist ethics, which must not surrender to or be drowned in the logic of bureaucratic elites.

There then begins the associated socialist mode of production. Labour is no longer commanded by an alien power but is transformed into a free and conscious self-activity on the part of the individual producer as part of the free association of labour directed toward the development of the individual's human essence or, at least, character. Meanwhile the means of production become the unmediated instruments of free and associated labour. In the associated mode of production understanding of nature continues to advance, drawing on and respecting ancient knowledges of gatherer-hunters and peasants, while production is based on a rational – that is to say, ecologically sound – regulation of the relationship between society and nature. This implies rational limits to production and consumption of wealth based on respect for the environment and the notions of material sufficiency and the importance of leisure time. In capitalism, the social character of the products of labour is posited only in exchange. Under socialism, community is posited prior to production. As a result of democratically informed planning, the products of labour will be known to be available to all those participating in social labour and even those who do not. The anticipation of demand is already built into the supply chains and sub-contracting of firms like Amazon and Walmart.

Labour time and the social distribution of time must be reduced to increase efficiency but also to maximise leisure. Under capitalism, increases in productivity are mediated by the law of value, whereas it is done in a conscious and controlled way under socialism. The necessary replacement of worn-out means of production, furthermore, is carried out under socialism by the planned relative overproduction of such means. In capitalism, this is done under conditions of competitive anarchy. Socialist bookkeeping also allows the long-term allocation of resources across different enterprises and projects on a basis that is more stable and secure than allowed by unplanned supply and demand. The social needs of the individual, not valorisation, determines necessary labour time. Disposable labour time becomes the measure of society's wealth. Wealth in the form of more time, in the form of use values rather than exchange values, in the form of unconstrained freedom, in the form of deeper human bonds and relationality, and in the form of access to ecologically healthy and intact territories, in the form of appreciation for human diversity and respect for the autonomy of the other, expands many times over. Labour time changes in that it is now directly social, freed of its previous antagonistic form, unconstrained by hierarchical organisation or the value form of the products it produces. Initially, each individual receives a token of her labour time, which is not money as it does not circulate. Eventually based on the high level of wealth, distribution no longer depends on labour time. Marx and Engels's formula, 'from each according to their abilities, to each according to their needs', is perhaps among the most far-reaching ethical statements ever produced. Though by now it has perhaps lost some of its original urgency through repetition, it remains a critical foundation of socialist ethics and a powerful reminder of what the current system doesn't even want to deliver. It also reminds us of the value of a civil service trained in poetry and ethics.

Whether we are in a time of revolutionary change or fascist reaction depends in large part on the actions of each of us amounting to a massive and organised collective rejection of the status quo in favour of a more just, sane, effective and egalitarian society. The concept mode of production is a critical tool in the arsenal of those of us who work towards such a change: It aims us at the real structural enemy, a system in which the needs of capital have precedence over the lives and needs of human beings. Any struggle for accommodation within capital, including those solely oriented towards placing more marginalised peoples into the boardrooms of capital, represent capitulations and a misdirection of energy. The concept mode of production allows us to take the measure over certain land-based environmental and anti-colonial struggles in a manner that allows for a specific understanding of why and how these struggles are critical challenges to capitalism. What follows is directed at certain lines of theory within the current historical conjuncture, in order to illustrate some other values of this critical intellectual tool, the concept mode of production.

2 There Is No Outside?

Certain streams of critical theory over the past five decades have subtly attempted to foreclose the discussion of revolutionary structural change, and indeed made the word revolution itself a pariah of intellectual conversation at least in the academy. A chain of thought that goes from Jacques Derrida's 'there is no outside the text' in *Of Grammatology* (1967), though a distinct methodological point on the philosophical level, has surely fed into or related to the similar pronouncement most widely known through Michael Hardt and Antonio Negri's 'there is no outside of empire' in their *Empire* (2000) and to more subtle versions of this in, for example, Judith Butler's 'if sexuality is culturally constructed within existing power relations, then the postulation of a normative sexuality that is "before", "outside", or "beyond" power is a cultural impossibility and a politically impracticable dream, one that postpones the concrete and contemporary task of rethinking subversive possibilities for sexuality and identity within the terms of power itself'.[1] These in part are inheritors of one line of thinking associated with Michel Foucault's politics of discursivity, a tepid social democracy that always settles for less, while dressing itself in the garb of theoretical radicality. We list these thinkers in part because of the vitality and reach of their work. But on this point we remain with the 'politically impracticable' dreamers: Empire has neither fully reached into the inner recesses of the psyche nor to the depths of the bush; the text remains indebted to the paper or body or land or face upon which it is written; normative forms of non-

1 Butler 1990, p. 30.

hierarchical sexuality can still be traced in the forms of gender relations and concomitant values that circulate among bush people.

There is no revolution without an outside: both the outside posited in imagination and the outside represented by distinct social forms that continue to persist across the chasm of modes of production. The current political moment demands the 'outside' of distinct human social forms and of very real but dramatically distinct possibilities. The tepid social democracy of a subversion that accepts the 'terms of power itself' does not amount to a political understanding of the strength of subversion itself: Subversion on our view amounts to deploying the tools of an unrelenting capitalist totalisation to preserve and reinforce the continued existence of a meaningful 'outside' itself. Rather than finding a comfortable place on the table that power has set, subversion involves reconstructing the place setting at a side table, or better on the floor!, where the whole menu starts with different premises.

Kulchyski's work on the Indian Act in Canada can serve as an example here. 'Indian' became a legal term of art in the united Upper and Lower Canada legislatures through the Civilisation Act of 1858. At that time, it was a broad term that encompassed anyone who wanted to think of themselves as Indian. After nationhood ('Confederation' in Canadian historical terms) a revised version of the Act, the Enfranchisement Act of 1869, started to restrict the definition by employing sex discrimination to remove women who married non-Indians from Indian legal identity. Through various amendments over the next decades (and a name change to the Indian Act), a set of criteria were established through which Indians could gain full citizenship rights. The term 'Indian' was defined simply as a person whose name was on a register kept by an official. The criteria to achieve so called 'full citizenship' included being able to speak and write English or French, for example. Importantly, the word 'status' or 'status Indian' never appeared or appears in the Indian Act. The idea was simple: 'Indians' (the term now is generally seen as racist; we use it in the historical and legal way it was and is used) were to have less rights than other citizens of Canada, and when they wanted to they could try to meet certain criteria to achieve those citizenship rights. Here, a totalising power, the Canadian state, deployed a legal mechanism in order to push for the erasure of original inhabitants, bush people, as a key element of its settler colonial clearing-the-way-for-capitalism mission. Interestingly, practicing agriculture was one of the criteria used – forcing bush people to become agriculturalists. In practice, something subversive took place. Indians did not try to achieve the criteria in order to get their names stricken from the register. The state was forced to use 'involuntary enfranchisement', such as with the women who married non-Indians to get 'Indians', to become 'Canadians'. And 'Indians' then started to distinguish between those who were not on the register and those who remained on it, calling the latter 'status Indians'. This was planned, organised, orchestrated, by no one. Being an Indian became a positive value for the subjects so defined, and a basis for their struggle to continue to practice their 'normative differences' against a totalising regime. Subversion used the terms of power to maintain a space 'outside the terms of power itself', as the basis for a revolutionary change still to come, as a way of maintaining an outside.

The revolutionary change still to come may be finding itself in the current historical conjuncture. If so, the thought that there is no outside will not serve it well. A return to the concept of mode of production remains a critical tool in the arsenal of revolutionary thought and practice, precisely because the change demanded must be for a better world, defined by the terms 'socialism' and 'communism'. Fredric Jameson, particularly in his work around utopian fiction, but also through his study of realism, and in both of those, his insistence on the value of the rupture aimed at socialism, offers a much more robust ground for truly revolutionary thought. Jameson's focus on changes within the materialist cultural frame of the capitalist mode of production is certainly a central element of his thought – the postmodernist thesis – and he does develop work insisting on the centrality of socialist futures. His work does not, however, spend significant effort on other existing modes of production, their place in history or in contemporary politics, or their role in challenging capitalism and presenting resources for socialist futures. This, we insist, remains a critical element in the revolutionary arsenal of thought. The bush and the undercommons, the mangrove and the autonomous zone, are actual or potential outsides of capital and empire that allow for politically impracticable dreamers to put their dreams into practice in this world, in the hope of providing a foundation for a better world. Such practices are an element of any revolutionary movement worth the name.

3 Totality and Totalisation

One peculiarity of the capitalist mode of production is the degree to which it is a totalising force. As Susan Buck-Morss points out, the idea of totalisation is a critical foundation of the dialectical materialist stream of Marxist theory. The French Marxist-existentialist Jean-Paul Sartre, a key thinker within this stream of thought, produced strong working definitions of totality and totalisation in his *Critique of Dialectical Reason*. These are worth recalling: 'a totality is defined as a being which, while radically different from the sum of its parts, is present in its entirety, in one form or another, in each of these parts, and which relates to itself either through its relations to one or more of its parts or through its relation to the relations between all or some of them'.[2] Sartre argues that 'totalisation has the same statute as the totality ... but it is a developing activity'.[3] Totalisation is not simply a matter of addition, but rather a matter of the spread of an underlying principle or force or structure. Sartre had the acuity to recognise that history is not simply about the spread of totalisation, but also of the many varied resistances to it, an issue to which we will return. For the moment, this element of domination deserves systematic attention.

More than any other mode of production, capitalism involves the attempt to reshape the whole of the world in its image, to impose its form of time, space, subjectivity, and knowledge on the other modes of production. It is a totalising form of forms. There are three interrelated underlying totalising forces that constitute capitalism. Two of these are explicitly theorised as totalising forces by Marx in *Capital*: the accumulation of capital and the expansion of the commodity form. The third is only treated as a totalising force nascently by Marx, though Marxist theorists, from Gramsci to Poulantzas, provide fertile theoretical reflections that point towards it: the capitalist state. A few words regarding each of these distinct but interrelated totalising forces will move this analysis towards a deeper understanding of particular conflicts between capitalism and the other modes of production in the contemporary world.

The accumulation of capital is the foundational totalising force that defines the capitalist mode of production, global history since the advent of modernism, and the contemporary period. Capital accumulation involves both original or primitive forms of accumulation, which remain active in, for example, extractive industries or accumulation by dispossession, and the money – commodity – money-prime (M – C – M′) formulation also developed by Marx to explain capital expansion. Capital itself is abstract wealth, distinct from any of the land, objects, ideas, labour power, or other both tangible or intangible social actualities or potentials that may constitute it. The accumulation of capital is associated with profit and with avaricious motivation but is not exclusively or necessarily linked to these, though it is not unreasonable to think of capital accumulation as the institutionalisation of greed, for example. While this is a form of totalisation that does involve addition, as a totalising force it is the logic of capital accumulation, a logic that places the growth of capital as a sacred and unquestioned necessity and the structural foundation of social being and the way in which the natural world is seen, that characterises it: This is the

2 Sartre 1978, p. 45.
3 Sartre 1978, p. 46.

underlying principle that every fibre of society must conform to and that the two other totalising forces extend. In effect, the most important decisions in the contemporary world that materially shape that world are made in board rooms by holders of capital, always in the interest of increasing their capital. In recent decades, fear of humans coming under the control of artificial intelligence (a la 'Hal' in Stanley Kubrick's *2001: A Space Odyssey*) has become at least a filmic, if not broader cultural trope. We believe this is a distorted reflection of what has already happened: The 'artificial intelligence' that controls us is no robot or computer though; it is the logic of capital to which we all must genuflect – even AI! It and all its bearers and representatives (we call them cheerleaders) are the quislings, enemies of what is human in humanity.

The commodity form is the single most powerful tool of capital accumulation but can be seen as a distinct totalising force. The commodity form reshapes the logic of every tangible and intangible element of social being, such that the logic of exchange value comes to dominate whatever use value can be said to attach to it. This expansion of the commodity form is a continuing process, and it is a critical way for capital to accumulate: By making more elements of social being commodified, capital dramatically expands the field within which it operates. The first chapter of *Capital* is devoted to this totalising force, which is totalising in exactly the way we have deployed that term: It is an underlying form that spreads not just to things, but to time, space, knowledge and to people who come to represent intellectual or labour power that produces additional values in the very process of being 'consumed'. Commodification is a concept dear to contemporary cultural studies scholarship, and can be a marker of a materialist approach to culture. We note as an aside the term is so widespread that some thinkers clearly haven't felt it necessary to do their homework: hence the even uglier term 'commoditisation'.

The state as a totalising force was only nascently theorised as such by Marx, in his understanding of the role of brute force as an element of primitive accumulation, for example. But the state played and plays a key role in creating the shifting conditions best suited to the accumulation of capital and the expansion of the commodity form, including the codifying and reshaping of space, time, subjectivity, knowledge and language. It is not only through brute force, repression or coercion that these changes are made, but through the busy work of defining time zones, demarcating spatial boundaries, circumscribing citizen rights and obligations, sponsoring research – that is, the many layers of integrating a spatially bounded social body with itself and with other such social bodies (nations). The state acts with a greater degree of intentionality than either of the other totalising forces, sometimes even to regulate or restrain the worst, self-destructive, impulses of capital itself. Support for the regime of capital accumulation is always the ultimate end of fascist and social democratic states alike, and all those in between. And, of course, the state does maintain ultimate control over the most powerful repressive forces within a given polity: When the busy working bureaucrats lose their grip on a particular problem, the police or military are always available as a more or less frequently used resource depending upon local circumstances and the temperament of the state leadership. It can be noted that the state as a totalising force precedes capitalism: The Qin dynasty in ancient China, for example, moved to homogenise a variety of features and have 'all under heaven' conform to its broad dictates. But capitalism harnesses and expands the totalising power of the state to such an unprecedented degree that totalitarianism becomes a tendential possibility to be exploited by every self-aggrandising cartoon Napoleon whose office is not large enough for his ego.

4 Totalisation, Colonialism, and Mode of Production

These three totalising forces are key in understanding the particular conflicts between distinct modes of production in contemporary times. What is called 'colonialism', in this view, is a historical and contemporary process whereby these forces are extended from a geographic area in which capital is sufficiently concentrated to be outward-looking to distinct peoples and areas that remain un- or less integrated. Each totalising force works in a slightly different way, and has differential impacts, depending upon whether they are acting upon the tributary mode of production – which shares some affinities with capitalism and can be said to be partially totalised – or the bush mode of production, which shares far less and involves much greater alterity.

The state operates in two modalities as a totalising force in colonial contexts. In its first modality it shows its repressive face. Brutal military conquests were the major leading mechanisms of state-established control of much of the world in the period of emerging capitalism. Sometimes, this took elements of the form of conquest that tributary states had deployed but the result would become more durable and more socially transformative as world capitalism gained in strength. Political domination created immediate wealth extraction of specific forms – gold! silver! slaves! – but also laid the groundwork for the other totalising forces, seemingly more benign but in the end far more consequential.

As the commodity form expanded geographically under the umbrella of state-sponsored colonialism, it transformed local products – sugar! rubber! coffee! oil! – into global commodities, and, critically, engaged local bodies first into directly subservient and expendable labour power (the unforgiveable, irreparable, repulsive systemisation of slavery into a globally sanctioned system) and eventually into immiserated forms of wage labour. But the commodity form also has a more subtle phase, as when it makes the bodies, lands or culture of the colonised themselves into commodities that can be 'freely' sold or purchased. In contemporary times, the exoticism of the other, and any of the goods or practices that can be connected to it, has become a valuable commodity, eating from the inside the meaning-value of the object or activity.

While these processes took place all in order to expand the field of capital accumulation, the latter also became a deliberate carrot tied to the repressive stick of colonialism. The colonised could become holders of small pockets of capital themselves, junior partners in their own subjugation, lulled by the impossible hope of themselves striding the world stage of conquest. Today, the state and capital both offer local partnership agreements everywhere where doubts about the impacts of their actions remain acute. This is a secondary level in which capital accumulation itself becomes a totalising force: In the first, it underwrites and is the reason for all other totalising processes, however brutal or apparently benign, in the second it offers itself with winning smiles to those small groups within the colonial world whose moral compass has become restricted to the demands of their own self-interest.

Finally, both the colonial state and the post-colonial state, having through basic brutality and immiseration created a necessary degree of social docility, expand the busy work of determining what time it is, what spatial zones will be used for what purpose, how children can be trained to the proper scale of obedience, what local insights, techniques, or expressive culture may find buyers. The polity is integrated into the global circuits of capital under intelligible forms of social interaction, and this integration is updated for the age of electricity, for the age of chemical production, for the age of digital circulation, for the age of every twist and turn of capital. This is then, in hushed and somber tones, portentously announced as the path to 'development', a secret only fully known by the mostly white bearers of progress and modernism.

While the struggle among the owners and workers of the means of production is a distinct driver of historical change in the capitalist world, and while workers themselves are no strangers to the insidious power of totalisation, what is outlined in the foregoing is the basis of a distinct and related political struggle against capitalism: the struggle to maintain vestiges of social forms that may be non- or anti-capitalist, the struggle to maintain a degree of autonomy from capitalism itself, the struggle for an 'outside' to empire within the pores of global capitalism at the present historical moment. The struggle is not aided in any measure when theorists who operate within the heart of empire proclaim it is already over. This is a version of the struggles that took place within Europe against the imposition of capitalist social forms, documented well by E.P. Thompson among many others. It is a struggle with distinct local permutations, contingencies, levels of engagement, intensities, solidarities. It is a struggle best understood as against the totalising overlay of one mode of production on the others, that plays a role in determining what specific historical shape a social formation will take. It is a struggle engaged in by bush people in Northern Canada, by Mayan farmers in southern Mexico, by 'tribal' peoples in rural India, by video artists in Greenland, hunters in Africa, by people almost everywhere who fish for their own food. One form their struggle takes, when they are not confronting the latest representatives of the latest giant job creating environment-destroying development project, is simply living their daily lives, daily routines, daily gestures, without ever referencing a clock. Immeasurable ethical damage will be done to the human species when only the most elite of corporate executives are allowed to throw away their luxury watches.

5 The Bifurcated Colonial Subject

One of the most significant implications of all the foregoing is that the colonial subject is bifurcated in a fashion that makes that particular term of a piece with the many other terms that elide the difference between the tributary and bush modes of production: tribal, Indigenous, aboriginal, traditional, pre-capitalist, colonised: All inscribe a sanctioned ignorance of what for materialist thought should be a fundamental distinction between gatherers and farmers or the bush and tributary modes of production. Just as important as the way in which the geographic grounds that colonialism had to overcome played a role in shaping its particular local history, so too the social ground it determined to level and the form of resistance offered by that social ground played a role. The manner in which totalising power operated and operates, and the manner in which it was and is resisted, were and are shaped by the way of life of those it relentlessly seeks to dominate.

Was Malinche so willing to work with Cortes because he appeared as an ally in a longstanding struggle her bush people had with the tributary Aztecs? Was a progressive liberal British ethos behind the mercantile relation they carried on for centuries with bush people in Northern Canada, or did it rather have to do with the impossibility of – and lack of any substantial reward for – carrying on a military conquest at that time in a part of the world that had no condensed sources of wealth (i.e., city-states)? Were longstanding conflicts between farmers and gatherer-hunters in Africa a key to understanding the internal conflicts that led the former to happily hunt and capture the latter, selling them as slaves to Europeans? Why did a relatively minor military skirmish in Bengal lead to consolidation of British imperial control there, if not for a top-heavy tributary regime? These historical events all have their own permutations and nuances, but at least to some degree explanation or understanding that does not attend the question of mode of production cannot produce an historical account of any compelling value.

The colonised is a bifurcated subject. Bush people are colonised. Tributary people are colonised. The specific form totalisation takes and the specific nature of resistance and collusion depend upon this difference. If Frantz Fanon thought that a national project in Algeria should have an Enlightenment dimension, and remained suspicious of traditionalists, perhaps that is because the Islamic (tributary) context he worked within supported pervasive social hierarchies that to his mind were indefensible. If Amílcar Cabral was far more sympathetic to traditionalists, perhaps that is because the sub-Saharan context included bush peoples whose substantive traditions were egalitarian (Cabral frequently used the word 'bush'). Both were anti-colonial thinkers in an African context, but the difference between them was worlds apart. Africa, the Americas and Asia all included this bifurcation, all homelands to people who live in different worlds. Ancient and feudal Europe also included it. Australia, the Arctic and the South Pacific seem to have entirely been the terrain of bush people. It should be noted that there are also egalitarian social forms among tributary peoples, whether nomadic Bedouins or other pastoralists, or in specific tributary contexts as, for example, can be found in contemporary Mayan towns and villages in southern Mexico or Guatemala.

In contemporary times these distinctions have been overlain by capitalism. Althusser and Poulantzas alike coined the term 'social formation' to account for this, though neither was much of a student of anti-colonial struggle. A social formation, in their account, is an existing historical or contemporary social space in which different modes of production operate at the same time. Dominant, vestigial and emergent modes vie for hegemony at different times and places, perhaps operating on distinct levels of social structure. The concept social formation is in our view a critical tool in the contemporary lexicon of anti-colonial discourse, though rarely deployed. Any national space may be seen as a social formation; its religion may be the vestige of a tributary spiritual institution, while the state-form may be entirely capitalist, for example. Capital itself can easily deploy the social differences and hierarchical structures of the tributary mode of production, and just as easily put its brand names on the social movements that overcome them, proudly celebrating its progressive social attitudes. The state everywhere plays a key role in managing these differential social variables, ensuring everyone gets to the meetings on time. Gayatri Chakravorty Spivak's corporate executive, ecologically-hip niece can bear these disjunctures in one body, as can any singular embodied subject.

The discussion around the politics of culture and identity in a global context can be reframed in this materialist manner. Cultural politics oriented to the survival of traditions can ask the question: What kind of traditions are we confronting? Traditions of patriarchal privilege in property relations are best swept into the dustbin of history. Gender egalitarian traditions, even in the context of a sharp gendered division of labour, may be intrinsically worth supporting and may inspire movements of gender equity within a dominant capitalist framework. The resistance to capitalist totalisation on the part of the working class as much as on the part of bush people or tributary people is a pervasive feature of contemporary cultural politics. Importing the terms of struggle between social classes to the particular conflicts between modes of production does more than a disservice: It can involve a dangerous attempt to co-opt people into a totalised space. The work of pseudo-Marxist Frances Widdowson is a striking example in the Canadian context of this form of idiocy: Calling on bush people to erase their differences and join the working-class movement for equality amounts to a cultural, ecological and in too many ways an actual death sentence.

6 Totalisation in the Capitalist World

The impact of capitalism on contemporary peasants and bush people is harsh and unrelenting. But so is its impact within the bounds of 'highly developed', 'modern', 'western', 'progressive' nations. Let Theodor W. Adorno's *Minima Moralia* here be seen as a description of everyday life in the suburban world, in which meaningful ethical relations are crushed under the brutal wheel of instrumental reason and the individualised, never-ending pursuit of self-gain. The logic of a possessive individualism that underwrites a culture of suspicion and of widespread socially generated narcissism makes any form of community an unsustainable nostalgic throwback, to such an extent that reputable thinkers can no longer contemplate the notion that meaningful communities are intergenerational. In this system, even the comparatively well off are forced to live with soul-crushing levels of anxiety and bitter antagonism and resentment towards their own family members. Instead of cherishing the extended lives of grandparents, some in the property-owning classes secretly wish them dead so they may finally have the means through inheritance to put into place long-cherished investment dreams or holiday travel plans. With no meaningful community to fall back on, the culture lurches from one quick fix to the next: Ephemeral communities of consumption replace intergenerational communities of production. And this is for the thin sliver of people to whom capitalism delivers some goods: the vanishing middle classes. The materially impoverished, often racialised and gendered, bottom of the social heap can only dream of having such problems as soul-destroying isolation and anxiety. Theirs is a world of precarious housing, precarious food, precarious health, in a context where being at the bottom is ever and always seen as a moral failing. In this world, there is little dignity at the top, if characters and charlatans the like of Trump can be found there; and even less at the bottom. Happiness and contentment are not generalised features of the world made in capital's image.

Both of the other modes of production relied on and developed mechanisms for the sustenance of intergenerational communities of production. Community itself is form of wealth, a fact that can only be recognised in this moment where the disappearance of community is everywhere presupposed – though not entirely successfully – by capital. On the affective level, community is what allows for the very possibility of a social engagement and connection that in turn produces meaningful contentment. Isolation is an endemic public health crisis created by the totalising spread of capital in a so-called 'first world' context. The lives we are permitted to live, even to aspire to, are impoverished by this deep structural fact. The toxic masculinity and authoritarianism that runs from the *Freikorps* proto-Nazis in interwar Germany to the contemporary militias of the United States also inflect family life to such an extent that feminised poverty is a necessary result as women flee the internalised brutality. Living in a deeply hierarchical social form means learned obsequiousness to those above and vicious command and control of those below, in the workplace as much as the family. It has become a social system that denies the very existence of the social, the most precious aspect of our species being.

7 Identities and Modes of Production

Social location and the attendant identities that get normalised or marginalised through this is the basis of what are called identity politics. Although the expression 'BIPOC' (black, Indigenous, people of colour) has become popular, the lens 'mode of production' allows for thinking the specificity of each of these. We have already emphasised the difficulties with the term 'Indigenous' for thinking about anti-colonial struggles of peasants versus those of bush people. The equality struggles of black americans do not easily provide concepts and practices that translate into the bush, where equality means assimilation. But those equality struggles are obviously not to be dismissed, and black thinkers have produced a growing host of analytical tools to challenge the specific forms of oppression they encounter. We note that research is called for to determine what cultural elements in the foraging strategies of slaves to supplement their subsistence or in the spiritual place of voudou in early revolutionary Haitian politics owe to bush practices of the source cultures (if they were bush rather than tributary sources). Mode of production inflected analysis can add a dimension of understanding to the plantation bifurcation of field slave versus house slave structure imposed on black bodies in the slave world, and perhaps to the strong sense of equality that inspires elements of the activist black leadership. We suggest that the term 'people of colour' has resonance as a unifying tool, but again note that the colonial subject is bifurcated in a way that needs careful attention.

Similarly, mode of production can speak to struggles of LGBTQ2S, and to ableism. The pervasive respect for personal autonomy, that is an element of bush culture, offers a strong resource for thinking an ethics that accounts for, respects, and indeed draws upon social difference. Gender and sexual identifications are fundamental building blocks of identity; a history founded upon the concept mode of production allows for recognition of the ways in which these subject positions are denaturalised and marginalised in the project of sustaining patriarchal and heterosexist property regimes. So, mode of production offers ways of understanding both the structure of these specific oppressions, as well as insights into worlds in which these oppressions are contradicted by everyday ethics. 'From each according to their abilities ...'.

Capitalist totalisation inflects all of these struggles. Capitalism as a system can function and indeed thrive on the back of any hitherto marginalised or denaturalised social group which gains an equality that amounts to being another abstracted body: labour power. The capitalist tendency to abstraction is also a tendency towards the abstract equality of the exploited and immiserated. Equal opportunity is not our slogan and cannot be our desire. A world in which black and female and differently abled and differently desired bodies circulate demands an entirely different form of ethics, one not based on grasping for better position within the hierarchy but rather based on attacking the presumption of hierarchy itself. Thinking at the level mode of production turns our attention to what really matters: not this or that marginalisation and the equal right to be exploited of that group, but the necessity of creating a world in which any such form of marginalisation is unthinkable.

8 Ecology and the Anthropocene

The concept of mode of production, carefully deployed, remains far more valuable than the current widespread taste for the 'Anthropocene'. The latter term repeats the fundamental error of leveling the major diversity of human lifeways into one universal category. It 'explains' the current ecological catastrophe by reference to the actions of all human beings over the course of all history. It is, simply put, far too blunt an instrument for the challenge of understanding who precisely is practically responsible for the crises of climate change and ecological degradation, levelling all human-ecology interactions as moments in a long duration that leads to the possibility of an environmental apocalypse to come. This then serves the interests of a capital-holding elite who can convince themselves and others that their actions are merely the latest iteration of age-old human processes. How can they help themselves, poor souls!

There should be no surprise when this form of thinking leads to 'solutions' like the notion of sparing some part (half?) of the earth as an ecological zone separated from humans, an idea propounded by E.O. Wilson in his wretched book *Half Earth*. This is, to be as clear as is required, as stupid a notion as has ever been suggested in the modern era. Most of the last large, intact, ecologically rich areas of the world are in fact occupied by bush people. These areas would be the basis of the half-earth that is to be depopulated: Arctic and Subarctic, jungles, deserts and mountainous lands that capital has not found a use for or that bush people have kept capital from taking. So, the very people who have sacrificed the most to defend their ecological homelands are to be forcibly (it would have to be forcible) removed from the areas they successfully defended, in the interest of an Imperial 'ecology'. Is there any doubt at all that the super-rich of the occupied half earth would not be able to bribe the occupied half to allow them luxury holidays in the newly 'pristine' global zones? Placing 'environmental' concerns, even global warming which does pose a threat to all forms of life on the planet in their current configurations, at the very centre of analysis is misguided. An eco-socialism worth the name understands that changing social and political structures is the only foundation for addressing the profound problems of ecological degradation and the specific problem of global warming. The artificial intelligence called capital accumulation is only interested in ecology to the extent it is exploitable. It has done a rather good job at that. Calling all human interactions with nature responsible for this catastrophe – as implied by the Anthropocene – is an appalling and unforgiveable failure of intellectual and political nerve.

The concept mode of production opens a space that understands how each mode of production has both a different concept of what its ecological context actually is (the work of an ancient lawgiver, the design of God, the result of long durational evolutionary processes, for example) and a very different set of practices and relations to those contexts. The idea of 'pristine wilderness', it should be noted, is an idea produced by modernist capitalism and is not a notion widely held by bush people or even by those in tributary contexts.

Bush people have a painstaking and intimate knowledge of the lands and waters they are in relation to. They do not leave these areas 'untouched' or 'pristine', but have made and do make significant changes (through widespread use of fire, for example) or 'tweaks' (building weirs, promoting certain plant or animal habitats, and so on). Bush people live off the wealth of the lands and waters they know intimately. That knowledge grows and deepens over centuries of occupation: The cultures are not static, but rather develop ethical practice, technical innovation, and ecological knowledge alike. The lands and waters stewarded by bush people have become a critical resource for a species that has, under the aegis of the capitalist mode of production, in a meagre few hundred years so degraded the ecological home of humanity that now it dreams of leaving for the stars it will never reach or removing bush people from those 'resource bases' they retain. Bush people in the past and present make, comparatively, very little impact that produces global warming, and are active protectors of the ecologies – Amazon, boreal forest – that are the best hope for reducing it.

In the tributary mode, land is dramatically reshaped to allow for animal husbandry or domestic plant growth. Forests are cleared, semi-deserts sometimes irrigated, rivers diverted, in a slow and unsteady 'progress' self-justified by the concept of 'civilisation' and frequently subject to setback or even collapse over centuries. Since the largest of these societies, in population terms, were vegetarian, their contributions to global warming were again comparatively small; there was little interest in huge herds of methane-producing cattle. If the world still existed with a mix of bush and tributary peoples, as it did for the vast majority of human history, global warming would not be taking place. Certainly, notions of dominion over nature were prevalent, and significant areas of the world were entirely deforested. But no single regime achieved the degree of global hegemony that would be required to entirely deforest, and the dynastic cycles of rising and falling empires or kingdoms meant there were lengthy periods where previously settled lands reverted to forest.

Clearly – so clearly it should barely need mention! – capitalism is responsible both for massive environmental degradation and for global warming. In a mere few hundred years since the arrival of the capitalist mode of production, nearly every corner of the world has been environmentally degraded beyond recognition. A massive extermination of an extraordinary variety of animal species has been taken place, reducing species variety to an unprecedented extent. A number of global ecological catastrophes loom, from the earlier threat to the ozone layer, to the insect apocalypse, to global warming. These are all directly a consequence, not of 'human nature' or a long durational human project called the Anthropocene, but of a mode of production that demands infinite accumulation in the context of a finite world. The capitalist mode of production is directly and entirely responsible for global warming. The notion of the Anthropocene is a lovely term that directs attention away from this obvious fact. We unhesitatingly toss it in the garbage can of theoretical nonsense. Similarly, we reject the concept of Capitalocene, a term which unnecessarily places the last few hundred years in a naturalist, geological sequence, thereby naturalising what must be seen as a very historically recent and even anomalous social project.

It can be noted that, yes, bush people spread globally and there is evidence that certain species may have been made extinct due to their actions. Farmers too, and pastoralists, were responsible for environmental impacts that likely lead to species extinctions and significant environmental degradations. But neither of these modes has had anything close to the level of ecological impact obviously a result of a meagre few hundred years of rapacious capitalism. The impacts of capitalism are of a qualitative magnitude vastly beyond whatever accusations can be levelled against both other modes. Discussion of the existential crises of global warming begins and ends with capitalism, and the idea of capitalism itself exists with any rigour as an expression of the concept mode of production. Global warming will not be solved by going to Mars or by depopulating half the planet. It can only be solved by ending the hegemony of capitalism over all other life ways, and by replacing it with something better. What stands in the way of any significant social action to end global warming are the owners and representatives of capital; the logic of capital trumps saving lives in a pandemic, trumps keeping the earth as a habitable home for many or most species, trumps keeping the earth a habitable home for humans, trumps working towards or arriving at a condition of global peace, trumps ensuring material security and individual dignity for every single human being.

9 Egalitarianism and Affluence: The Socialism to Come

The ultimate fate of our species now depends upon a rapid foundational structural change away from having the needs of capital accumulation at the structural limit of all decision making towards what Marx called the dictatorship of the proletariat, a deeply democratic structure capable of putting the needs of people first. 'Rapid foundational structural change' is a polite term for revolution. The globally dominant mode of production needs to give way to a new globally dominant form, called socialism. In other words, a new world needs to be born out of the pores of this existing one, drawing on what can be learned from now less dominant modes, and this birth cannot happen too soon.

In our view, going too far down the path of imagining this new world, while a lovely daydream, will not play a strong role in achieving the goal. A few things can be added to what has already been said, and we leave the utopian imagining for minds less tainted by the traumas of today than our own. The core elements of the mode of production, both the forces and the relations of production, will need to be restructured. The pace and nature of technological change needs to be yoked by ethical concern: a discussion of what and whether in regard to each technological 'advance' is one critical element of a socialism that will deserve its name. It is time to turn social hierarchy into the nightmare we awaken from. The relations of production must be founded on a profoundly egalitarian ethos: not a homogenising egalitarianism where everyone is the same, but an equality in which the distinct quality of each matters. This is well captured in Marx and Engels's astounding and immeasurably valuable formulation, which we cannot repeat enough: 'from each according to their abilities and to each according to their needs'.

It is our particular view, here, that there must be room in the socialist world to come for each of the other modes of production. Bush people must continue to steward their lands. Egalitarian farmers and nomads must have room to pursue their plots and shepherd their herds. Markets too, and enterprise, belong in this world, though it will be a world without billionaires. Perhaps those who achieve and succeed may be worthy of twice what the average person has, but little more. All of these peoples will have access to the latest technologies and play a role in the decision-making structures and live contemporary lives. Diversity of modes of production, within the hegemony of socialism, will offer a ground to meaningful cultural difference.

It is our contention that the values that circulate among bush peoples, which include respect for the autonomy of the other, egalitarianism, participatory democracy, generalised reciprocity, and ecological relationality and caring, these are a practical foundation for the values a socialism that deserves the name would promote. Bureaucratic structures do not lean in towards these values: The state will play a critical revolutionary role in counterbalancing the current power of capital in the transitional phase. But the goal must not be to replace a capitalist elite with a socialist elite, and structures must be put in place to ensure that forms of ossification in social structure do not take place.

Rancière's notion of election by lot has much to commend it and is surprisingly suited to the politics of hunting bands.

A final but important point in this brief sketch: The socialism to come is not to be defined by generalised poverty. The egalitarianism we urge is not one in which all are poor, but rather one in which all are affluent. However, that affluence can come in the many forms of 'to each according to her or his or their needs'. Along with bush people, we see wealth in the form of a meaningful community which emotionally and materially supports each of its members, wealth in the form of access to lands that have been allowed to maintain their gentle or explosive beauty, wealth in the form of the richness and variety of tasks that can be contributed to the social good, wealth in the form of the freedom that individual bodies are permitted and permit themselves in work and play, wealth in the form, finally and critically, of the time each person may take to choose their path, love their parents and lovers and children, express their most creative dreams and live their lives. The wealth we speak of is the wealth of the good life, not calculated in the accountancy of capital and power, but lived in contentment and fulfillment. We contribute these words to the project of bringing into being a world in which these forms of wealth are available to everyone.

10 Source Note

Paresh Chattopadhyay has been one of our key sources for thinking about socialist possibilities as articulated in the work of Marx and Engels. The theory of totalisation we offer owes its inspiration to Jean-Paul Sartre's *Critique of Dialectical Reason*, in which the analysis of serial social collectives and the theory of colonialism also afford strong conceptual lines of thought for materialist analyses. Moten and Harney's *The Undercommons* offers an inspiring range of ideas that act as a corrective to and vastly surpass the 'there is no outside' mantra of too much contemporary 'theory'.

References

Adorno, Theodor 1991, *Minima Moralia*, translated by E.F.N. Jephcott, New York: Verso.

Althusser, Louis 1971, *Lenin and Philosophy*, translated by Ben Brewster, New York: Monthly Review Press.

Amin, Samir 1974, 'Modes of Production and Social Formations', *Ufahamu: A Journal of African Studies*, 4, 3: 57–8.

Anderson, Perry 1974, *Passages from Antiquity to Feudalism*, London: New Left Books.

Anderson, Perry 1974, *Lineages of the Absolutist State*, London: Verso.

Anievas, Alexander and Kerem Nisancioglu 2015, *How The West Came To Rule: The Geopolitical Origins of Capitalism*, London: Pluto Press.

Arrighi, Giovanni 1994, *The Long Twentieth Century: Money, Power and the Origins of Our Times*, London; New York: Verso.

Aston, T.H. and C.H.E. Philpin (eds.) 1985, *The Brenner Debate; Agrarian Class Structure and Economic Devlopment in Pre-Industrial Europe*, Cambridge; London: Cambridge University Press.

Astarita, Carlos 2011, 'Peasant-Based Societies in Chris Wickham's Thought', *Historical Materialism*, 19, 1: 194–220.

Bagchi, Amiya Kumar 2005, *Perilous Passage: Mankind and the Global Ascendancy of Capital*, New Delhi; Oxford; New York: Oxford University Press.

Banaji, Jairus 2010, *Theory As History: Essays On Modes of Production and Exploitation*, Leiden: Boston.

Bellamy-Foster, John, Hannah Holleman and Brett Clark 2020, 'Marx and Slavery', *Monthly Review*, 72, 3: 96–117.

Benjamin, Walter 1978, *Illuminations*, translated by Harry Zohn, New York: Schocken Books.

Bhabha, Homi 1994, *The Location of Culture*, New York: Routledge.

Blackburn, Robin 1997, *The Making of New World Slavery: From the Baroque to the Modern 1492–1800*, London; New York: Verso.

Bois, Guy 1985, 'Against the Neo-Malthusian Orthodoxy', in *The Brenner Debate; Agrarian Class Structure and Economic Devlopment in Pre-Industrial Europe*, edited by T.H. Aston and C.H.E. Philpin, Cambridge; London: Cambridge University Press.

Bois, Guy 1992, *The Transformation of the Year One Thousand: The Village of Lournand From Antiquity to Feudalism*, Manchester: Manchester University Press.

Brenner, Robert 1976, 'Agrarian Class Structure and Economic Development in Pre-Industrial Europe', *Past & Present*, 70, 170: 30–75.

Brody, Hugh 1977, *The People's Land*, Harmondsworth: Penguin Books.

Brody, Hugh 1983, *Maps and Dreams*, Harmondsworth: Penguin Books.

Brody, Hugh 1987, *Living Arctic*, Vancouver: Douglas and McIntyre.

Brody, Hugh 2000, *The Other Side of Eden*, Vancouver: Douglas and McIntyre.

Buck-Morss, Susan 1989, *The Dialectics of Seeing*, Cambridge: MIT Press.

Butler, Judith 1990, *Gender Trouble*, New York: Routledge.

Cabral, Amílcar 1979, *Unity and Struggle*, translated by Michael Wolfers, New York: Monthly Review Press.

Calinicos, Alex 2004, *Making History: Agency, Structure, and Change in Social Theory*, Leiden: Brill.

Chattopadhyay, Paresh 2021, *Socialism in Marx's Capital: Towards a Dealienated World*, Palgrave Macmillan.

Clastres, Pierre 1983, *Society Against the State*, New York: Zone Books.

Cohen, G.A. 2000, *Karl Marx's Theory of History: A Defence*, Princeton, N.J.: Princeton University Press.

Coulthard, Glen 2014, *Red Skin, White Masks*, Minneapolis: University of Minnesota Press.

Debord, Guy 1983, *Society of the Spectacle*, translated by Ken Knabb, London: Rebel Press.

De Sainte Croix, Geoffroy 1981, *The Class Struggle in the Ancient Greek World*, Ithaca: Cornell University Press.

Derrida, Jacques 1976, *Of Grammatology*, translated by Gayatri Chakravorty Spivak, Baltimore: Johns Hopkins UP.

Diamond, Stanley 1987, *In Search of the Primitive; a Critique of Civilization*, New Brunswick: Transaction.

Dobb, Maurice 1963 [1946], *Studies in the Development of Capitalism*, New York: International Publishers; London: Routledge & Kegan Paul.

Engels, Friedrich 1986, *The Origin of the Family, Private Property and the State*, Toronto: Penguin.

Fanon, Frantz 1966, *The Wretched of the Earth*, translated by Constance Farrington. New York: Grove Press.

Foucault, Michel 1979, *Discipline and Punish*, translated by Alan Sheridan, New York: Vintage Books.

García Mac Gaw, C. 2015, 'The Slave Roman Economy and the Plantation System', in *Studies on Pre-Capitalist Modes of Production*, edited by L. Da Graca and A. Zingarelli, Leiden; Boston: Brill.

Godelier, Maurice 1978, 'The Concept of the Asiatic Mode of Production and Marxist Models of Social Evolution', in *Relations of Production: Marxist Approaches to Economic Anthropology*, edited by David D. Seddon and Frank Cass.

Godelier, Maurice 1979, 'Epistemological Comments on the Problems of Comparing Modes of Production and Societies', in *Toward A Marxist Anthropology: Problems and Perspectives*, edited by Stanley Diamond, The Hague; Paris; New York: De Gruyter.

Graeber, David and David Wengrow 2021, *The Dawn of Everything: A New History of Humanity*, Canada: McClelland and Stewart.
Gramsci, Antonio 1980, *Selections from the Prison Notebooks*, translated by Quinton Hoare and Geoffrey Nowell Smith, New York: International Publishers.
Haldon, John F. 1993, *The State and the Tributary Mode of Production*, London; New York: Verso.
Haldon, John F. 2015, 'Mode of Production, Social Action, and Historical Change: Some Questions and Issues', in *Studies on Pre-Capitalist Modes of Production*, edited by L. Da Graca and A. Zingarelli, Leiden, Boston: Brill.
Haldon, John F. 2009, 'The Byzantine Empire', in *The Dynamics of Ancient Empires*, edited by Ian Morris and Walter Scheidel, Oxford: Oxford University Press.
Hardt, Michael and Negri, Antonio 2001, *Empire*, Cambridge, MA: Harvard University Press.
Harman, Chris 2008, 'An Age of Transition? Economy and Society in England in the Later Middle Ages', *Historical Materialism*, 16, 1: 185–199.
Harney, Stefano and Moten, Fred 2013, *The Undercommons*, New York: Minor Compositions.
Harvey, David 1992., *The Postmodern Condition: An Enquiry Into the Origins of Cultural Change*, Cambridge, MA: Blackwell.
Harvey, David 2005, *A Brief History of Neoliberalism*, Oxford: Oxford University Press.
Heller, Henry 2006, *The Bourgeois Revolution in France 1789–1815*, New York: Berghahn.
Heller, Henry 2011, *The Birth of Capitalism*, London: Pluto.
Heller, Henry 2014, 'Marx's *Capital* as History', *International Critical Thought*, 4, 1: 38–52.
Heller, Henry 2017, *The French Revolution and Historical Materialism: Selected Essays*, Leiden: Brill.
Heller, Henry 2018, *A Marxist History of Capitalism*, London: Routledge.
Heller, Henry 2019, 'Class and Class Struggle', in *The Oxford Handbook of Karl Marx*, edited by Matt Vidal et al., Oxford: Oxford University Press.
Hill, Christopher 1940, *The English Revolution*, London: Lawrence & Wishart.
Hill, Christopher 1948, 'The English Civil War Interpreted by Marx and Engels', *Science and Society*, 12, 1: 130–156.
Hill, Christopher 1967, 'Pottage for Freeborn Englishmen: Attitudes to Wage Labour in Sixteenth and Seventeenth Century England', in *Socialism, Capitalism and Economic Growth*, edited by C. Feinstein, Cambridge: Cambridge University Press.
Hill, Christopher 1969, *Industry and Empire: From 1750 to the Present Day: The Penguin Economic History of Britain. Vol. 3*, Harmondsworth; New York: Penguin.
Hill, Christopher 1980, 'A Bourgeois Revolution?', in *Three British Revolutions: 1641, 1688, 1776*, edited by J.G.A. Pocock, Princeton: Princeton University Press.
Hill, Christopher 1984, *The World Turned Upside Down: Radical Ideas During the English Revolution*, London: Penguin Books.

Hobsbawm, E.J. 1962, *The Age of Revolution: Europe 1789–1848*, London: Weidenfeld & Nicholson.

Hobsbawm, E.J. 1975, *The Age of Capital 1848–1875*, New York: Charles Scribner's Sons.

Hobsbawm, E.J. 1987, *The Age of Empire 1875–1914*, New York: Vintage.

Hobsbawm, E.J. 1994, *The Age of Extremes: The Short History of the Twentieth Century, 1914–1991*, New York: Vintage Books.

Holoroyd, Josh 2020, 'Marxism, the State, and the Tributary Mode of Production', *In Defense of Marxism*, available at: https://www.marxist.com/marxism-the-state-and-the-tributary-mode-of-production.html

James, C.L.R. 1938, *The Black Jacobins: Toussaint L'Ouverture and the San Domingo Revolution*, London: Seckert & Warburg.

Jameson, Fredric 1988, *The Political Unconscious*, Ithaca: Cornell University Press.

Jameson, Fredric 1991, *Postmodernism or, The Cultural Logic of Late Capitalism*, Durham: Duke University Press.

Kulchyski, Peter 2005, *Like the Sound of a Drum*, Winnipeg: University of Manitoba Press.

Kulchyski, Peter 2010, 'subversive identities: indigenous cultural politics and canadian legal frameworks, or, indigenous orphans of the state', *e-misferica*, available at: https://hemisphericinstitute.org/en/emisferica-62/6-2-essays/e62-essay-ubversive-identities-indigenous-cultural-politics-and-canadian-legal-frameworks-or.html

Kulchyski, Peter 2016, 'Hunting Theories: Totalisation and Indigenous Resistances in Canada', *Historical Materialism*, 24, 3: 1–15.

Kulchyski, Peter 2018, *Report of an Inquiry into an Injustice: Begade Shutagot'ine and the Sahtu Treaty*, Winnipeg: University of Manitoba Press.

Kulchyski, Peter 2018, 'Bush/Animals', in *Animals and Animality in the Literary Field*, edited by Molly Hand, Bruce Boehrer and Brian Massumi, Cambridge: Cambridge University Press.

Kulchyski, Peter 2019, 'Bush/revolution: theses on the challenges that gatherers and hunters pose to dominant structures', *Third World Quarterly*, 41, 8: 1406–1420.

Kulchyski, Peter 2023, 'Marx For Primitives', *Rethinking Marxism*, 35, 4: 564–82.

Leacock, Eleanor Burke 2008, *Myths of Male Dominance*, Chicago: Haymarket Books.

Leacock, Eleanor and Richard Lee (eds.) 1982, *Politics and History in Band Societies*, Cambridge: Cambridge University Press.

Lemarchand, Guy 2011, *Paysans et seigneurs en Europe: une histoire compare, XVIe–XIXe siècle*, Rennes: Presses Universitaires de Rennes.

Li, Minqi 2021, 'China: Imperialism or Semi-Periphery?', *Monthly Review*, available at: https://monthlyreview.org/2021/07/01/china-imperialism-or-semi-periphery/

Manning, Brian 1991, *The English People and the English Revolution*, London: Bookmarks.

Manning, Brian 1996, *Aristocrats, Plebians and Revolution in England 1640–1660*, London; Easthaven; Connecticut: Pluto Books.

Marx, Karl and Friedrich Engels 1975 [1846], *The German Ideology: Critique of Modern German Philosophy*, in Marx and Engels, *Collected Works*, Volume 5, London: Lawrence & Wishart; New York: International Publishers.

Marx, Karl and Friedrich Engels 1975b [1859], *Introduction to a Critique of Political Economy*, in Marx and Engels, *Collected Works*, Volume 29, London: Lawrence & Wishart; New York: International Publishers.

Marx, Karl and Friedrich Engels 2004, *The Communist Manifesto*. Peterborough: Broadview Editions.

Marx, Karl 1973, *Grundrisse*, New York: Random House.

Marx, Karl 1974, *The Revolutions of 1848: Political Writings, Volume 1*, edited by David Fernbach, New York: Vintage Books.

Marx, Karl 1976, A *Contribution to the Critique of Political Economy*, edited by Maurice Dobb, New York: International Publishers.

Marx, Karl 1977, *Capital, Volume I*, New York. Random House.

Marx, Karl 1977–81, *Capital*, 3 Vols., translated by Ben Fowkes, New York: Vintage.

McNally, David 2020, *Blood and Money: War, Slavery, Finance, and Empire*, Chicago: Haymarket Books.

Mészáros, István 1995, *Beyond Capital: Toward A Theory of Transition*, New York: Monthly Review Press.

Moore, Jason 2015, *Capitalism in the Web of Life*, New York: Verso.

Patterson, Orlando 2018, *Slavery and Social Death: A Comparative Study*, Cambridge, MA: Harvard University Press.

Pomeranz, Keith 2000, *The Great Divergence: China, Europe, and the Making of the Modern World Economy*, Princeton: Princeton University Press.

Poovey, Mary 2008, *Genres of the Credit Economy*, Chicago: University of Chicago Press.

Post, Charles 2003, 'Plantation Slavery and Economic Development in the Antebellum Southern United States', *Journal of Agrarian Change*, 3, 3: 289–332.

Poulantzas, Nicos 1980, *State, Power, Socialism*, translated by Patrick Camiller, London: Verso.

Rancière, Jacques 2014, *Hatred of Democracy*, New York: Verso.

Rousseau, Jean-Jacques 2011, *The Basic Political Writings*, translated by Donald Cress, Indianapolis: Hackett Publishing.

Sahlins, Marshall 1972, *Stone Age Economics*, Chicago: Aldine-Atherton Inc.

Sartre, Jean-Paul 1978, *Critique of Dialectical Reason, Volume 1*, translated by Alan Sheridan-Smith, London: New Left Books.

Scheidel, Walter 2019, *Escape From Rome: The Failure of Empire and the Road to Prosperity*, Princeton: Princeton University Press.

Sewell, William H. 2021, *Capitalism and the Emergence of Civic Equality in Eighteenth-Century France*, Chicago: University of Chicago Press.

Stavrianos, Leften 1981, *Global Rift: The Third World Comes of Age*, New York: Harper Collins.

Thompson, E.P. 1968, *The Making of the English Working Class*, Harmondsworth, England: Penguin.

Thompson, E.P. 1993, *Customs in Common*, New York: The New Press.

Wallerstein, Immanuel 1974, *The Modern World-System*, New York: Academic Press.

Wickham, Chris 2005, *Framing the Early Middle Ages: Europe and the Mediterranean 400–800*, Oxford: Oxford University Press.

Wickham, Chris 2008, 'Productive Forces and the Economic Logic of the Feudal Mode of Production', *Historical Materialism*, 16, 2: 3–22.

Williams, Eric Eustace 1944, *Capitalism and Slavery*, Chapel Hill, N.C.: University of North Carolina Press.

Wilson, E.O. 2016, *Half Earth*, New York: Liveright Publishing.

Wolf, Eric R. 1982, *Europe and the People Without History*, Berkeley: University of California Press.

Wolf, Eric R. 1999, *Peasant Wars of the Twentieth Century*, University of Oklahoma Press.

Index

ability and ableism 2, 3, 4, 27, 83, 84, 85, 137
abstraction 14, 20, 27, 32, 38, 40, 74, 75, 83, 92, 102, 108, 109, 110, 116, 118, 129, 137
Adorno, Theodor 135
  Minima Moralia 135
affluence 10, 11, 12, 13, 29, 88, 108, 142
Afghanistan 29
Africa 7, 23, 28, 34, 41, 42, 47, 54, 63, 64, 68, 71, 75, 92, 118, 133, 134
Agamben, Giorgio 18, 21
Algeria 23, 134
Althusser, Louis 1, 17, 20, 21, 22, 64, 66, 72, 134
Americas 7, 22, 23, 31, 34, 41, 47, 76, 92, 134
Amin, Samir 10, 21, 59, 61, 62, 63, 67, 70, 71, 78, 80
Ancien Régime 65, 121
Anderson, Perry 70
anthropocene 8, 11, 138, 140
anthropology 3, 7, 20, 21–2, 26, 33, 68, 81, 84, 93, 94, 96, 97, 98
Arctic 22, 91, 108, 134, 138
Asia 7, 23, 28, 34, 54, 63, 67, 68, 92, 134
Asiatic mode of production 19, 21, 62, 63, 67–8, 69, 73, 74, 77, 78, 80
Astaria, Carlos 71
Australia 22, 134
Aztec 28, 65, 69, 133

Babeuf, Gracchus 49
Banaji, Jairus 17, 70, 78, 80
Bedouins 134
Bengal 134
Benjamin, Walter 13, 37
Bhabha, Homi 24
BIPOC 1, 8, 136
Blackburn, Robin 74–5
Black Lives Matter 121
Bois, Guy 17, 70, 71, 72
Bolivia 13, 25, 48, 121
Bolshevik Party 55, 56
bourgeois 40, 51, 52, 53, 100, 124
bourgeoisie 9, 17, 40, 43, 44, 46, 49, 50, 51, 57, 100, 124
Brenner, Robert 17, 61
Buck-Morss, Susan 128
Buddhism 28, 66, 69, 77
bush mode 7, 11, 13, 19, 21, 23, 24, 25, 27–9, 32, 33, 37, 42, 54, 62, 81–98, 101, 102, 104, 106, 107, 111–12, 114, 115, 131, 133
Butler, Judith 126

Cabral, Amilcar 23, 134
Caesar, Julius 14
California 5
Callinicos, Alex 6
Calvino, Italo 83
Canada 5, 34, 52, 121, 122, 127, 133, 135
capitalism and capitalist mode 1–3, 6–7, 9, 10, 11–12, 13, 17–21, 25, 27, 28–30, 32–33, 36–61, 62, 64, 66, 67, 69, 70, 72, 74–76, 78–79, 80, 82, 83, 84, 86, 87, 92, 93, 95–97, 102–05, 108–10, 114–16, 118, 120–22, 124–26, 127–28, 129, 131, 132, 134, 135, 136–37, 139, 140
  late capitalism 43, 58, 83, 84
  merchant capitalism 42, 43–44, 45–48, 51
  monopoly capitalism 43, 53–54, 58
capitalist accumulation 7, 8, 9, 12, 20, 21, 27, 28, 29, 38, 39, 40, 41, 42, 43, 44, 47, 51, 53, 58, 64, 66, 75, 104, 105, 109, 110, 116, 123, 129, 130–31, 132, 138, 140
  crises 1, 2, 8, 9, 38, 57, 59, 60, 72, 110, 120, 122–23
  origins 41, 73
  relation 37–8, 39, 41, 55, 57, 60, 73
  state 2, 8, 20, 27, 28, 38–39, 43, 44, 46, 53–54, 57–58, 59, 77, 95, 103, 104, 114, 121–24, 127, 129–31, 132, 134
Chattopadhyay, Paresh 122, 142
China 13, 22, 25, 28, 32, 42, 43, 44, 49, 55–8, 60, 64, 65, 67, 69, 72, 76, 78, 92, 120, 121, 131
Christianity 28, 45, 66, 117
church 28, 45, 49, 50, 57, 66, 70, 77
classes 2, 3, 4, 10, 11, 13, 14, 17, 19, 22, 24, 27–8, 33, 38, 44, 45, 48–9, 50–4, 56, 58, 59, 61–3, 65, 68–9, 70, 71–3, 76–9, 83, 103–04, 105, 114, 121–24, 135
class struggle 3, 8, 9, 17, 19, 32, 48, 51, 53–54, 57–8, 65, 68–9, 72–4, 76–7, 79, 121

Clastres, Pierre 84
climate change 2, 3, 138
Cluniacs 70
Cohen, G.A. 17
colonialism 23, 30, 41, 42, 44, 46–8, 54, 95, 131, 132, 133, 142
commodity 8, 19, 27, 39, 40, 62, 75, 118, 129–30, 131–32
communist party 18, 56, 57, 58, 68
Confucian 28, 69, 77
consumerism 58, 60
Corn Laws 51
Cortes, Hernan 133
Coulthard, Glen 23
covid-19 2, 9, 79
Cuba 13, 21, 25, 29, 49, 56, 58, 76
culture 7, 10, 11, 14, 16, 18, 23–4, 25, 27, 28, 29, 33, 48, 49, 54, 66, 81, 83, 89, 90, 93–94, 99, 102, 106, 113–14, 116, 118, 130, 132, 135–36, 137

Daoism 28, 69, 117
Dene 14
De Gouges, Olympe 49
Deleuze, Gilles 102
democracy 2, 8, 10, 24, 25, 36, 38, 52, 55, 57, 60, 85, 97, 122, 123, 125, 126–127, 131, 140, 141
Derrida, Jacques 21, 26, 94, 126
  Of Grammatology 126
Descartes, René 46
dialectics 7, 17, 21, 22, 82, 98, 104, 115, 128, 142
Diamond, Stanley 98

ecology 1, 3, 8, 9, 14, 27, 29, 31–4, 36, 39, 48, 52, 57, 67, 79, 83, 87–8, 90–3, 95, 96, 99, 107–08, 111, 122–23, 125, 135, 138–41
egalitarian 5, 6, 8, 11, 12, 13, 22, 23, 28, 29, 33, 34, 83–86, 88, 90, 91–92, 97, 108, 112–13, 115, 126, 134, 135, 140–42
English East India Company 64
Engels, Friedrich, 1, 3, 6, 11, 19, 20, 26, 35, 37, 73, 81, 96, 98, 100, 122, 125, 141, 142
  The Communist Manifesto 19, 35, 100
  The Origin of the Family, Private Property and the State 19
environment 3, 5, 8, 37, 53, 59, 60, 104, 105, 120, 123, 125, 126, 133, 138, 139, 140
equality 13, 40, 49, 51, 52, 83, 97, 135, 136–37, 141
Eurocentrism 78, 80
Europe 7, 21, 26, 28, 31, 32, 34, 39–40, 41–9, 51–4, 57, 62–5, 67, 69, 70–1, 72–3, 75, 78, 92, 120–21, 133, 134
exploitation 19, 32, 37, 39, 43, 44, 46, 48, 59, 66, 71, 72, 74–5, 76–7, 78, 79
  absolute 43, 47, 59
  relative 43, 47, 59

factories 38, 47, 51
Fanon, Frantz 23, 134
fascism 2, 9, 56, 57, 60, 122, 124, 125, 131
feminism 7, 13, 49, 81, 96, 98, 136
finance 2, 31, 47, 53, 57, 59, 64, 75, 121
forces of production 7, 8, 14, 15, 16, 18–9, 36–7, 49, 51, 52, 53, 58, 60
Foucault, Michel 21, 126
France 44, 46, 48, 49, 50, 52, 53, 54, 57, 64, 65, 76, 121, 135
French Revolution 40, 48–9, 50

gender 2, 3, 11, 20, 22, 25, 27–8, 45, 58, 81, 83, 84, 85, 92, 96, 97, 98, 115, 127, 135, 137
Germany 64, 136
Global South 2, 56, 58–9, 60, 105
global warming 2, 9, 120, 138–40
Godelier, Maurice 17, 80
Graeber, David 4–5, 6, 91–2, 97
  The Dawn of Everything 4, 91
Gramsci, Antonio 1, 8, 129
Great Britain 14
Greece 28, 73
Greenland 133
Guarani 14
Guatemala 134

Haiti 49, 50, 61, 75, 137
Haldon, John 66, 76–8, 80
Hardt, Michael 126
  Empire 126
Harman, Chris 17
Harney, Stefano 142
  The Undercommons 142
Harvey, David 61, 119
Haudenosaunee 31, 107, 122
Hindu 28, 66, 117

history 3, 7, 9, 11, 13–6, 19, 21, 22, 23, 26, 29, 36–7, 42, 56, 58, 61, 62, 64, 67, 68, 69, 72, 76, 78, 79, 81, 83, 90, 93–4, 96, 98, 110, 116, 118, 128, 129, 133, 135, 137, 138, 139
Hobbes, Thomas 82, 83
Holroyd, Josh 78, 80
hunting 5, 6, 10, 11, 19, 20, 22–3, 25, 26, 29, 34, 41, 42, 46–7, 62, 84, 87, 89, 91, 95, 98, 99, 107, 108, 111, 113, 115, 142

imperialism 36, 43, 53, 54, 56–7, 58, 60, 123
Inca 21, 28, 69
India 23, 28, 32, 42, 44, 64, 67, 69, 72, 121, 133
Indian Act (Canada) 127
Indians (American) 83, 127–28
Indigenous 1, 7, 8, 12, 21, 22, 23, 47, 48, 54, 64, 93, 94, 99, 107, 133, 136
industrial revolution 36, 40, 50–1, 52, 59, 65
inequality 2, 4, 9, 12, 13, 20, 36, 37, 43, 59, 60, 78, 114, 115, 120–21, 122, 123
Islam 23, 28, 66, 77, 117, 134

Jameson, Fredric 7, 22–3, 26, 96, 97, 100, 101, 119, 128
  The *Political Unconscious* 22
Japan 14, 28, 52, 53, 57, 76

Khaldun, Ibn 23
  Muqaddimah 23
Kubrick, Stanley 130
  2001: A Space Odyssey 130
Kulchyski, Peter 115, 127

labour 18, 19, 21, 22, 25, 27, 29, 32, 34, 36, 37–43, 45–50, 51–2, 54, 55, 58, 59, 64, 65, 68, 70–6, 77, 84, 89, 104, 108, 110, 115, 122, 124–25, 129, 130, 132, 135, 137
  free 40, 50, 51–2, 76
La Malinche 133
landlords 31, 37, 38, 39, 44, 51, 57, 62, 64–8, 71–3, 77, 79, 124
Latin America 41, 42, 46, 47, 54, 64, 67, 75, 121
Leacock, Eleanor 22, 81, 98
Lebanon 121
Le Chapelier Law 50
Lee, Richard 22, 81, 98
Lenin, Vladimir Illich 18, 55, 56

Levi-Strauss, Claude 21, 94
  Tristes Tropiques 94
LGBTQ2S 1, 4, 8, 137
liberalism 49, 52, 57, 122, 133
Luther, Martin 40

Mac Graw, Carlos Garcia 74
Mandan 107
Mandela, Nelson 23
manufactures 41, 42, 43, 44, 47, 51, 53, 68, 71
Marx, Karl 1, 3–4, 6, 7, 11, 14–17, 19–21, 29, 34, 35, 37, 38, 40, 42, 51, 55, 62, 67–8, 73, 74–5, 81, 86, 89, 94, 100, 110, 113, 122, 125, 129, 130, 140, 141, 142
  Capital 35, 75, 110, 129, 130
  The Communist Manifesto 19, 35, 100
  A Contribution to the Critique of Political Economy 16, 20, 34–5
  Economic and Philosophic Manuscripts of 1844 122
  Ethnological Notebooks of Karl Marx 19
  The German Ideology 15, 17, 35
  Grundrisse 14, 19, 35, 122
Marxism and Marxist 1, 2, 3, 4, 5, 6, 7, 8, 13, 14, 17, 21, 23, 55, 78, 81, 94, 99, 100, 128, 129, 135
Mauss, Marcel 21, 88
Maya 28, 69, 133, 134
McCarthy, Cormac 34
  The Road 34
Mészáros, István 55–6, 57
Mexico, 29, 49, 133, 134
Middle East 7, 44, 64, 67, 68, 121
mode of production 1, 3, 4, 5, 6, 8, 10–17, 18–23, 24, 26, 27, 30, 31, 32–4, 35, 36, 37, 39, 49, 62, 67, 73, 74, 78, 79, 87, 93, 96, 97, 100–02, 104, 106, 111, 113, 116, 118, 120, 126, 127–29, 131, 133, 134–35, 136, 137, 138, 140, 141
modernity 19, 23, 24, 26, 29, 32, 37, 49, 54, 58, 81, 90, 93–8, 103, 119, 120, 128, 129, 132, 139
Moten, Fred 142
  The Undercommons 142

nationalism 52, 54, 58, 60, 122
Negri, Antonio 126
  Empire 126
neoliberalism 2, 9, 43, 56, 58–9, 79, 121

neolithic 5, 31, 65, 71
  bias 82, 94, 97
  break 11, 19, 31, 32, 62, 81, 91, 92, 97
Newton, Isaac 46
nomadic 7, 28, 33, 67, 69, 81, 106, 107, 108, 110, 134, 141
nomadism 29, 81, 82, 87, 106, 107, 108
North America 48, 75, 107

October Revolution 55, 124

Pakistan 121
Pandemic 2, 9, 36, 39, 120, 123, 140
patriarchy 4, 6, 11, 22, 26, 28, 30, 50, 66, 78, 106, 114, 117, 135, 137
Patterson, Orlando 73, 75
Pontiac's Rebellion 48
population 5, 25, 32, 43, 44, 45, 47, 54, 57, 60, 76, 91, 96, 97, 106–08, 120, 121, 123, 139
Poulantzas, Nicos, 1, 8, 20–1, 100, 119, 129, 134
  State, Power, Socialism 20, 119
poverty 11, 12, 13, 36–7, 43, 54, 123, 136, 142
primitive accumulation 39, 41, 43–45, 47, 75, 95, 114, 130
productivity 43, 51, 58, 59, 117, 125
progress 7, 11, 19, 26–8, 36, 42, 46, 49, 57, 66, 68, 93, 97, 108, 109–10, 116, 118, 132, 133, 134, 135, 139
property 4, 6, 11, 17, 19, 20, 25, 28, 37, 38, 39, 45, 46, 55, 57, 66, 77, 81, 86, 87, 91, 92, 103–06, 108, 114, 116, 118, 123, 135, 137

Qin dynasty 14, 39, 60, 69, 118, 131

race 2, 3, 27, 73, 83
racism 7, 13, 26, 47, 50, 54, 75, 121, 127
Ranciere, Jacques 25, 142
Reagan, Ronald 2
relations of production 7, 14, 16, 17, 18, 36, 41, 49, 60, 74, 76–7, 92, 94, 100, 101, 123, 141
religion 15, 25, 28, 31, 45, 62, 63, 66, 69–70, 77–8, 116, 117, 134
Reform Act (1832) 51
revolts 48, 49
revolution 1, 4, 8, 9, 10–11, 12, 16–7, 22, 29, 32, 40, 46, 49, 51, 52, 55, 58, 72, 78, 92, 100, 101, 105, 110, 114, 120, 122, 123–24, 125, 126–27, 128, 141
  American 48, 49
  Chinese 29, 49, 55–7, 58
  Cuban 29, 56, 58
  English 61
  French 40, 49, 50, 52, 54–5, 61, 79
  Haitian 49, 50, 75, 137
  industrial 36, 40, 50–2, 59, 65
  Russian 49, 54, 55, 56, 57, 124
  Vietnamese 13, 29, 49, 56, 58
  scientific 46, 47
Rome 14, 28, 65, 73
Rousseau, Jean-Jacques 4, 20, 21, 81, 82, 96, 98

Sahlins, Marshall 22, 23, 71, 81, 88, 89, 98
Sartre, Jean-Paul 4, 98, 102, 128–29, 142
  Critique of Dialectical Reason 98, 128, 142
scarcity 10–11, 36, 37, 52, 97, 98
sexuality 2, 3, 13, 25, 27, 45, 58, 82, 83, 84, 85, 114, 126–27, 137
silk road 60, 121
Sima Qian 69
slavery 5, 25, 28, 38, 41, 42, 46, 47, 50, 51, 52, 62, 64, 66, 70–2, 73–6, 79–80, 93, 131, 132, 134, 137
Smith, Adam 40
social hierarchy 10–13, 20, 23, 27, 28, 30, 31, 66, 83, 88, 91, 92, 96, 103–06, 109, 110, 114, 141
socialism 8, 20, 36, 42, 52, 55–6, 57, 58–60, 96, 97, 119, 122, 123–25, 128, 138, 140–42
social relations 6, 8, 15, 16, 17, 28, 40, 41, 66, 78, 81, 105, 118
South Pacific 22, 23, 34, 69, 134
Soviet Union 13, 54–6, 58, 59
spatiality 7, 14, 18, 100, 101, 102–05, 106–07, 110, 119, 130, 132
spectacle 2, 27, 28, 29, 66, 90, 102, 104, 111
Spinoza, Baruch 46
spirituality 24, 28–9, 66, 81, 89–90, 91, 95, 104, 106, 107, 110–12, 114, 116–17, 134, 137

Spivak, Gayatri Chakravorty 29, 135
Stalin, Joseph 54, 56
state 2, 4, 5, 7, 10, 11, 15, 19, 20, 27, 31, 37, 38–40, 41, 43–4, 45, 46, 48–9, 52–3, 54, 55, 56, 57, 58, 59, 60, 62, 63, 64, 65–7, 68–9, 71–2, 74–5, 76–7, 79, 91, 92, 95, 103, 104, 106, 114, 115, 119, 120, 121, 123, 124, 127, 129, 130–31, 132, 133, 134, 141
  absolutist 44, 48, 63, 64
subarctic 91, 107, 138
subversion 95, 127, 128
surplus 14, 19, 21, 37–9, 40, 41, 47, 51–2, 55, 56, 60, 62, 64, 65–7, 68, 71, 73–75, 76–7, 98
Ste-Croix, G.M.E. de 73
Sweden 13, 2

Tacitus, Publius Cornelius 82
technology 18, 28, 43, 60, 72, 90, 100, 105
temporality 7, 14, 18, 108–110, 113
Ten Hours Act (1847) 51
Thatcher, Margaret 2
Thompson, E.P. 2, 38, 61, 119, 133
  Customs in Common 119
totalisation 7, 8, 21, 30, 39, 93, 102, 118, 127, 128–29, 131, 132, 135, 137, 142
totalising 8, 10, 14, 19, 24, 27, 32, 37, 41, 93, 95, 100, 118, 127, 128–33, 136
town and country divide 66, 104
tributary mode 5, 7, 13, 19, 21, 24, 28, 29, 30, 32, 33, 37, 38, 42, 49, 50, 54, 60, 62–4, 65–7, 69–70, 71–4, 76–7, 78–9, 80, 91–3, 96, 101, 102, 105–06, 110, 112, 114, 116, 117, 120, 131, 133, 134, 139
Trump, Donald 120, 124, 136
Túpac Amaru 48
Twain, Mark 99

uneven development 42, 46, 123
unions 2, 50, 54
United Kingdom 2
United States, 2, 21, 49, 51, 52, 53, 54, 57, 58–60, 76, 121–22, 136

Value (economic) 19, 38, 40–1, 51, 52, 59, 75, 76, 118, 125, 130
  surplus value 2, 38, 40, 41, 51, 52, 56, 60, 75
Venezuela 13, 25
Vietnam 13, 29, 49, 56, 58

war 41, 54, 57, 58–60, 62, 73, 78, 98, 106, 111, 121
Wengrow, David 4, 6, 91, 92, 97
  The Dawn of Everything 4, 91
Wickham, Chris 17, 70, 71, 78, 80
Widdowson, Frances 135
Williams, Eric 74
Wilson, E.O. 138
  Half Earth 138
witches 45
Wolf, Eric 21, 29, 62, 63, 67, 78, 80
  Europe and the People Without History 21
Wollstonecraft, Mary 49
women 4, 29, 45, 49, 57, 78, 84–85, 117, 127, 136
Woolf, Virginia 33
  To the Lighthouse 33
workers 4, 25, 27, 31, 37–39, 44–5, 46, 48, 49, 50, 51–2, 54, 56, 59, 60, 74, 75, 83, 84, 89, 97, 104, 121, 124, 132
world market 41, 47, 60

Xi Jinping 57

Zimbabwe 13

www.ingramcontent.com/pod-product-compliance
Lightning Source LLC
LaVergne TN
LVHW011031160826
845780LV00026B/220
* 9 7 9 8 8 8 8 9 0 8 9 0 7 *